Secrets UNDERGROUND

North America's Buried Past

Elizabeth MacLeod

annick press

toronto + new york + vancouver

We acknowledge the support of the Canada Council for the Arts, the Ontario
Arts Council, and the Government of Canada through the Canada Book
Fund (CBF) for our publishing activities.

ONTARIO ARTS COUNCIL
CONSEIL DES ARTS DE L'ONTARIO
50 YEARS OF ONTARIO GOVERNMENT SUPPORT OF THE ARTS
50 ANS DE SOUTIEN DU GOUVERNEMENT DE L'ONTARIO AUX ARTS

Cataloging in Publication
MacLeod, Elizabeth, author
        Secrets underground : North America's buried past / Elizabeth
MacLeod.

Includes bibliographical references and index.
ISBN 978-1-55451-631-5 (bound).—ISBN 978-1-55451-630-8 (pbk.)

        1. Caves—North America—Juvenile literature. 2. Tunnels—North
America—Juvenile literature. 3. Underground areas—North America—
Juvenile literature. I. Title.

GB601.2.M33 2014   j551.44'7   C2013-906699-3
                          624.19

Distributed in Canada by:
Firefly Books Ltd.
50 Staples Avenue, Unit 1
Richmond Hill, ON L4B 0A7

Published in the U.S.A. by Annick Press (U.S.) Ltd.
Distributed in the U.S.A. by:
Firefly Books (U.S.) Inc.
P.O. Box 1338
Ellicott Station
Buffalo, NY 14205

Printed in China

Visit us at: www.annickpress.com

Secrets
UNDERGROUND

With love to Karen Virag, a wonderful writer,
editor, and friend—and a truly beautiful flower!
—E.M.

CONTENTS

ACKNOWLEDGMENTS

It's no secret that I love working with photo researcher Sandra Booth and designer Sheryl Shapiro! Thank you both for your creativity and skill, and for being so fun to work with. Many thanks also to wonderful editor Chandra Wohleber for helping me dig deep to make this the best book possible. Special thanks as well to managing editor Katie Hearn, copy editor Linda Pruessen, proof-reader Heather Sangster, marketing manager Brigitte Waisberg, and the entire Annick team.

For help with my research, thank you to Douglas MacLeod, Chair, RAIC, Centre for Architecture, Athabasca University; Andrew Mott, The Royal Exchange, San Francisco; and the librarians of the Toronto Public Library system, especially those at the Leaside Library and Toronto Reference Library.

Thanks always to Dad, John, and Douglas. And lots of love to Paul for his support, help with photography, and so much more.

SECRETS BURIED DEEP UNDERGROUND

Brush past the cobwebs, duck under the crumbling archway, and discover some of history's greatest hidden subterranean mysteries. Deep down, down, down below the earth's surface is a completely different world—sometimes terrifying, often baffling, and always fascinating.

The air is murky and dank, and the darkness is velvety thick as tiny creatures scuttle past. "Underground" is a place of spine-tingling mysteries and surprises that lurk concealed and forgotten, just waiting to be rediscovered. Eerie sounds drift through the air and inky shadows obscure and confuse.

You can find these buried secrets right across North America—beneath buildings and busy city streets or deep in sheltering mountains:

▮ Which cave in West Virginia concealed a Civil War secret?
▮ What closely guarded equipment lies deep below Grand Central Terminal in New York City?
▮ Which prairie town covers a network of tunnels that once hid victims of racism—and illegal liquor?
▮ Could the biggest city in North America have disappeared without a trace?
▮ How can an entire sailing ship be completely buried without anyone noticing?
▮ What did the U.S. government hide beneath an exclusive resort?

And why do these lost subterranean passages, spaces, and caves matter? Why not let their old, broken-down contents stay hidden and forgotten? Well, historians and experts who are curious enough to investigate the gloom—and brave enough to venture into the unknown—probe these mysteries to discover what it was *really* like to live in long-ago times.

Delving belowground can also uncover the answers to cryptic puzzles. For instance, thanks to underground investigations, historians now know how the Confederate side in America's Civil War managed, against impossible odds, to supply its soldiers with ammunition. And deep below one of North America's largest cities, deductions have led to the likely identification of a mysterious train car.

The discoveries made deep underground can help us understand our own past, explaining why some parts of the country have developed the way they have. They've also brought to light the profound misery and human cost of discrimination, and have explained why areas in one west coast city are especially prone to earthquake damage. Uncovering abandoned places underground even gives us insight into the future: from helping us prepare for possible natural or man-made disasters to bracing an ancient city, such as Mexico, against further damage to its very foundations.

In these forgotten tunnels and caves you can meet brave soldiers, greedy fortune seekers, and terrified immigrants. The shadows may also conceal mighty leaders, inscrutable officials, and ruthless spies. So get ready to take a sometimes moldy, often muddy walk through history to discover what amazing things are hidden underground. Who knows—some might be waiting right under your feet!

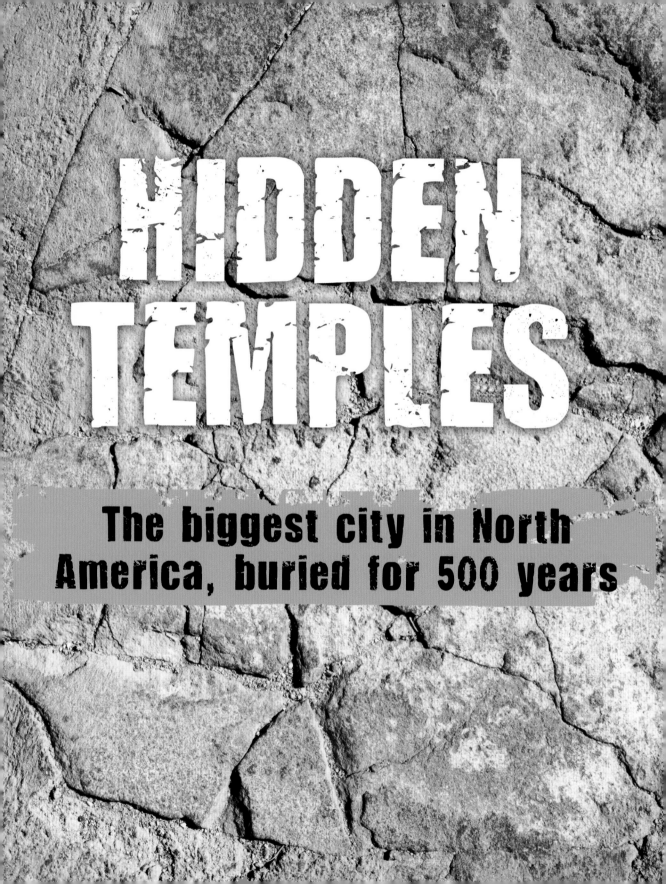

HIDDEN TEMPLES

The biggest city in North America, buried for 500 years

THE PLACE:
MEXICO CITY, MEXICO

THE BIG EVENT:
THE SPANISH CONQUEST
OF MEXICO (1519–1521)

Wiping the tears from her eyes, the Aztec woman gazed at the ruins of her beloved city. It was one of the largest cities in the world and now it was demolished. She had watched thousands of brave Aztec warriors fight the Spanish invaders, but they had lost. Utterly. Her husband and sons were dead, slaughtered in the streets. Thousands of other wounded Aztecs cried out and moaned their dying breaths.

Their beautiful city of massive stone temples and gorgeous palaces lay in pieces, savagely destroyed. Even worse, the Spanish soldiers vowed to erect their new buildings right on top of the ancient Aztec structures. The invaders were determined: when they were finished, there would be no trace of the incredible city. It would be as if it had never existed.

The woman turned and sadly hurried away, before the Spanish could come after her. If only she had known that the foreign conquerors wouldn't really succeed in obliterating her city. Not entirely, not forever …

THE BEGINNINGS UNCOVERED

An Island Home

For 200 years, the Aztecs had been searching for a homeland. They'd been told by their god of war, Huitzilopochtli (pronounced *wee-tsee-loh-POHCH-tlee*), that they should settle at the place where they saw an eagle on a cactus eating a snake. So they kept moving throughout the area now known as Mexico, searching for that cactus with the eagle and the snake.

Finally, in 1325, the Aztecs arrived at Lake Texcoco. Many other tribes had come and gone from the shores of the lake, but no one had ever really lived here. However, the Aztecs looked out at a small swampy island in the middle of the lake and saw the eagle, the cactus, and the snake, just as Huitzilopochtli had foretold. They knew they had found their home.

AN EAGLE ON A PRICKLY PEAR HOLDING A SERPENT

The legend about how the Aztecs chose the site for their capital city of Tenochtitlán—where Mexico City stands today—is very important to the country's history. When Mexico's flag was designed in 1821, an image representing the legend was placed in the center. Take a close look and you'll see the eagle holding a serpent, perched on a prickly pear cactus.

The bars of color on the flag have special meanings too. They represent hope (green), unity (white), and the blood of Mexico's heroes (red).

Many people confuse the Aztec, Inca, and Maya cultures. The Aztec empire was at its peak between the 1300s and 1500s, and focused around the area where Mexico City is now. Many Mexicans are descended from this group.

The Maya empire was at its greatest long before the Aztecs—from about 2000 BCE to 250 CE—and was located in the jungles of Belize, Guatemala, Honduras, and the Yucatan. Their descendants still live in those areas.

At its height in the early 1500s, the Inca empire stretched along the west coast of South America from Ecuador to northern Chile. It reached its peak slightly later than the Aztec empire did. Many Inca now live in Peru.

The Largest City in the World

The Aztecs named the island Tenochtitlán (pronounced *tay-NOTCH-tee-TLAHN*)—it means "among the prickly pears growing among rocks" in the Aztec language—and built a city there. It became the largest and most powerful city in the area that's now known as Mexico and Central America, and was one of the largest in the world by the 1500s. It was at the heart of where Mexico City is today.

The island city was connected to the mainland by beautiful wide causeways and bridges. The place where the cactus stood was sacred, so that's where the Aztecs built their main temple: the Huei Teocalli (pronounced *way-TAY-oh-kawl-ee*), or Templo Mayor in Spanish. The temple was shaped like a vast stepped pyramid, and there were shrines at the top.

The Aztec empire grew, gradually dominating the other tribes in the area. But the powerful empire made a lot of enemies along the way, and they would come to regret it.

UNITED STATES

MEXICO   Yucatan

Mexico City   BELIZE
GUATEMALA   HONDURAS
NICARAGUA

ECUADOR→

PERU→

CHILE→

JUST THE FACTS

The New World

In 1492, explorer Christopher Columbus opened up a "new world" for European countries when he arrived in the Americas. Spain was financing his voyages and it wasn't long before other Spanish soldiers and adventurers sailed to what's now known as Mesoamerica—it includes today's countries of Mexico, Belize, Nicaragua, and more. These men were called conquistadors, which means "conquerors" in Spanish.

Hernán Cortés was a pale and sickly child but grew up to become a tough leader.

The Spaniard Hernán Cortés arrived in Tenochtitlán in late 1519, leading a group of conquistadors. Cortés was brave, ruthless—and cunning. He was supposed to claim the Aztecs' land for Spain. But Cortés was more interested in their gold and wealth.

As Cortés marched to Tenochtitlán to meet with Moctezuma, the leader of the Aztecs, he made alliances with other Native tribes. These were the tribes the Aztecs had controlled for so long, so they were happy to side with any group that was planning to stand against them.

The Return of the Serpent God Quetzalcoatl?

On November 8, 1519, the conquistadors had their first glimpse of Tenochtitlán. Towering pyramids and beautiful painted stone carvings, all in a style they'd never seen before, overwhelmed them. Lush gardens scented the air and nobles lounged gracefully in stone courtyards. "Some of the soldiers," wrote one, "even asked whether the things that we saw were not a dream."

This incredible temple in Tenochtitlán celebrated Huitzilopochtli, the Aztec god of war.

Moctezuma was also stunned by his first glimpse of the conquistadors. He and his people knew the prophesies about the feathered serpent god

Quetzalcoatl (pronounced *Kett-sul-KOE-ay-tle*). The stories said he would one day come back in human form—and would come from the eastern ocean. That was how the Spaniards had come.

The great deity Quetzalcoatl was bearded, like these men. As well, Aztec priests had predicted he would come back to his people around the same year the conquistadors arrived. Could the god have returned?

Did the Aztecs Really Think Cortés Was a God?

Today, no one is sure whether Moctezuma and his people truly believed Cortés was Quetzalcoatl. Some historians now think Cortés cleverly started the rumors that he was a god to intimidate the Aztecs. And perhaps the Spaniard didn't understand the Aztec culture. It's true that Moctezuma dressed Cortés in precious jewelry and a feathered, gem-encrusted headdress. But what the Spanish leader didn't know was that this was how the Aztecs typically dressed a victim who was about to be sacrificed.

ROYALLY ANGRY

Never heard of the Aztec leader Moctezuma? That's because over the many years since he lived, his name was mispronounced and changed to Montezuma. He reigned in Tenochtitlán from 1502 to 1520, and it was during this time that the Aztec empire reached its maximum size. The name Moctezuma means "he who is angry in a noble way" in Nahuatl, the Aztec language.

Today, no one is really sure how Moctezuma died. Some accounts say Aztecs stabbed him or stoned him because he helped the Spanish. Other accounts say the Spanish killed him once he could no longer control his people.

Moctezuma was so important that he was guarded by 200 chieftains and only a few were allowed to speak to him.

Experts believe that this large feather head-dress once belonged to Moctezuma.

A FOREST DEEP IN THE MUD

It's hard to believe an entire forest could be buried and forgotten, but scientists say that's what happened in Nantucket Sound, Massachusetts. Not only that, but the buried forest may help solve a puzzle that has confounded experts for years.

The trees became submerged under 1.8 meters (6 feet) of mud, thanks to changing ocean levels due to melting glaciers after the Ice Age. The forest, which is more than 5,000 years old, likely holds clues to the mystery of how people arrived in North America. Experts are also hoping to find tools there to help explain how people lived back then.

Moctezuma probably wasn't giving in to Cortés—he was actually sending the opposite message. In the Aztec culture, being overly polite was Moctezuma's way of showing his incredible power and importance. In fact, the Aztec leader had allowed the Spaniards to enter Tenochtitlán only so that he could discover their weaknesses.

And use that knowledge to crush them.

Massacres and Mayhem

Trouble really began when Cortés received word that some of his men had been killed by Aztecs on Mexico's coast. Cortés grabbed Moctezuma as his hostage.

The Aztecs quickly realized they couldn't trust the Spanish. Stories had reached the Native people of a ruthless slaughter by the Spanish during their march to Tenochtitlán. Cortés wrote that, to teach one of the other Native groups a lesson, "We fought so hard, in two hours more than 3,000 men were killed." Thanks to their steel weapons and firearms, the Spanish could fight and kill in a way that the Aztecs, with their wooden clubs and spears, could hardly imagine.

In June 1520, Cortés's men massacred 10,000 Tenochtitlán nobles. The rest of the people rebelled and furiously attacked

SOLDIER OF 1585.

The gun this conquistador is firing is an arquebus (pronounced *ARR-kwuh-bus*), an early version of the musket.

the conquistadors. In the terrible bloodshed, Moctezuma was killed and the Spanish had to fight their way out of the city. They slashed and blasted a desperate escape across the bridges that connected it to the main land. Many of the conquistadors drowned because they tried to swim across, but were too weighed down with stolen gold.

The Spaniards fled, but they continued to kill the people of Tenochtitlán with a secret weapon they didn't even know they had: the disease smallpox. The Aztecs had never been exposed to the viral disease and, unlike the Europeans, had no resistance to it.

Experts estimate that as much as half of the city's population died an agonizing death from smallpox between 1520 and 1521. Over the next 60 years, about 80 percent of the Aztec population in the area died of smallpox.

The end of the city of Tenochtitlán was near.

HIDDEN

Last Days of Tenochtitlán

The wounded, diseased Aztecs were too weak to defend their island city. Cortés and his men soon took command of the bridges and causeways linking it to food and supplies: the Spaniards starved the sick and dying people of Tenochtitlán. On August 13, 1521, after destroying most of Tenochtitlán, the Spaniards conquered the city.

Now they started another killing spree. But this time, their target was the city itself. They toppled the incredible pyramids, burned the buildings, and hacked off the carvings. The huge city lay in ruins.

What hadn't already been demolished was dismantled or

buried as the Spaniards removed all traces of the Aztecs. The savage conquerors ransacked the temples, including the beautiful Templo Mayor. They snatched the gold statues and other precious objects. Cortés ordered the entire capital city destroyed.

Covering Up the City

Next, the Spanish leader decreed that a Spanish-style city be built over the rubble, so all traces of Tenochtitlán would be buried deep below the ground. Where the Templo Mayor had stood, there would now be a Spanish (Catholic) church. (It would later be the Mexico City Metropolitan Cathedral.) Despite how important the Templo Mayor had been to the Aztecs, it was so totally destroyed that everyone completely forgot its exact location.

Even the city's name was destroyed. From now on, it would be called Mexico City.

The Spaniards' guns and disease decimated the Aztec population. Soon there were few left to remember

VILLAGES LOST UNDERWATER

Tenochtitlán was buried by enemy invaders. But there are many other ways cities can be submerged and abandoned. The creation of the St. Lawrence Seaway in 1958 resulted in the flooding and burying of ten villages in Ontario, Canada. The seaway allows large ships to sail from North America's Great Lakes to the Atlantic Ocean.

The flooding was planned and in the months leading up to it, families and businesses were moved to nearby communities. Once a nearby dam was opened, it took just four days for the towns to disappear.

The conquistadors forced the Aztecs to build Mexico City on the ruins of Tenochtitlán.

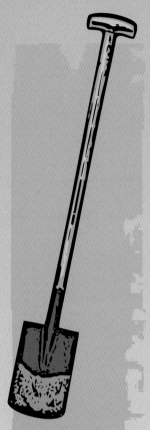

what lay beneath the new buildings of Mexico City. The temples and palaces of Tenochtitlán were wrecked and obliterated. It wasn't long before their remnants were buried and forgotten. Tenochtitlán lay lost and abandoned far below the rock and dirt for hundreds of years.

THE SECRET REVEALED

A Shocking Discovery

The electrical worker yelled and dropped his tools in shock. But the jolt he'd received wasn't electrical. He was digging for underground cables about 2 meters (6 feet) below the street, near the main square in Mexico City, when he suddenly hit something unexpected and solid. Quite solid.

Something very large was under the pavement. The worker had discovered a stone disc more than 3.25 meters (10.7 feet) in diameter, or big enough to fill a medium-sized room. It was 30 centimeters (12 inches) thick and weighed 8.5 tonnes (8.5 tons).

But even more interesting was what was carved on the stone. Surrounded by ornate swirls and decorations was a moon goddess. Archaeologists who quickly arrived on the scene knew this meant the stone was likely from a temple. It may have had a very gruesome purpose: experts said it might have stopped sacrificed bodies from rolling out of the pyramid-shaped temple.

Almost 500 years had passed, but on February 25, 1978, what Cortés and his men had tried so hard to bury impossibly deep underground and eliminate forever had been found. For years archaeologists had deduced that there might still be traces of Tenochtitlán hidden far below the streets of Mexico City, and now these workers had uncovered the city's Templo Mayor. Could the whole ancient city be waiting underground?

The discovery of this stone disc in 1978 led to the excavation of the Templo Mayor.

When archaeologists began studying the area, they found many artifacts, most in surprisingly good condition. It was such an incredible find that the Mexican government even agreed to tear down about 13 buildings in the area to make way for more digging.

Unearthing Tenochtitlán

Since 1978, archaeologists have found more than 7,000 ancient objects in the area, ranging from clay pots and masks to animal skeletons and precious knives made of obsidian (shiny black rock from volcanoes) and flint (hard quartz stone). Today they can all be seen in the Templo Mayor Museum that now stands nearby.

In October 2006, workers made another incredible find in the same neighborhood. They discovered a 4-meter-long (13-foot-long) carved stone that may have covered the tomb of an Aztec leader. Although the huge stone was broken into four pieces, it still showed traces of red, white, blue, and black paint, which is unusual after so many years.

This is one of the ritual obsidian knives uncovered from the Templo Mayor.

During the centuries this huge carved stone lay beneath Mexico City, it cracked into four parts.

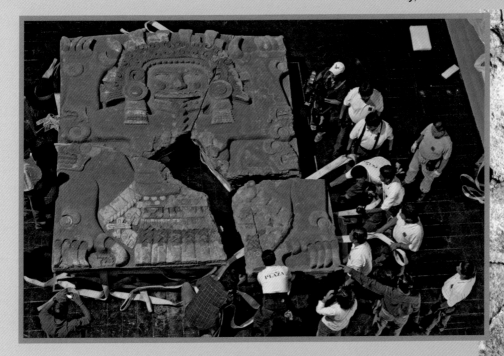

THAT SINKING FEELING

With a population of about 21.2 million, Mexico City is North America's largest city. But it's built on the drained bed of Lake Texcoco and too much groundwater has been removed from the lake. Its soft base is collapsing—in just the past 100 years, the city has sunk as much as 9 meters (30 feet) in places.

That's not all. The layers of clay under the city are different thicknesses, so the city is sinking unevenly. That makes subway walls crack, sidewalks buckle, and buildings tilt.

Unfortunately, the vast stone was found near an area of Mexico City where so many people live that it's unlikely any of the nearby buildings can be removed to allow for more digging.

Will the Rest Stay Buried Forever?

Up to 78 Aztec temples are concealed deep belowground by Mexico City's buildings, roads, and plazas. Experts know exactly where about 50 of them are, but only the temple discovered by the electricians has been mostly restored. It is thought that as little as 0.2 percent of the archaeological remains of Tenochtitlán have been excavated.

It's likely all the rest—by far the majority—will have to remain buried. There may not be enough money to uncover more before they are buried farther by new roads and skyscrapers. Many secrets of Tenochtitlán will have to stay hidden, perhaps never to be seen again.

Excavation continues at the Templo Mayor site in Mexico City.

BURIED SAILING SHIPS

The town built on top of boats

THE PLACE:
SAN FRANCISCO, CALIFORNIA

THE BIG EVENT:
THE CALIFORNIA GOLD RUSH
(1848–1855)

"Get back here, you wretched crew!" shouted the ship's captain. "Return this instant, swine!"

But the captain was talking to himself. All the members of his crew—every single one—were already long out of earshot. They had jumped ship as soon as they'd reached San Francisco, some before the passengers had even alighted. And none were coming back.

Once, the captain's vessel had sailed the world's oceans. Like hundreds of other ships, its timbers had carried the sailors and dreamers who made their way to San Francisco to get rich quick when gold was found in California.

"You lily-livered landlubbers," the captain raged. "What's going to happen to my ship?"

With no crews, what would be the fate of any of these vessels? It's hard to believe that whole ships can be abandoned, forgotten, and lost. But that's exactly what happened.

However, sometimes things that sink into oblivion have a way of becoming uncovered—often when least expected.

THE BEGINNINGS UNCOVERED
River of Gold

Gold was probably the last thing on John Sutter's mind when he put men to work building a sawmill on his property, about 210 kilometers (130 miles) northeast of San Francisco. But not for long!

After the workers finished the mill, they dug a channel so water from the nearby American River could run under the mill wheel and turn the giant saw blade. The next morning, January 24, 1848, the workers were back on the job. But they couldn't believe their eyes: "I shall never forget—my eye was caught with the glimpse of something shining in the bottom of the ditch," remembered James W. Marshall, the foreman.

The river had washed away the sand and gravel under the mill wheel—and revealed a bright gold nugget! Marshall ran to John Sutter to show him the find. They soon discovered there was more where that nugget came from.

Sutter begged his men to keep the find quiet; he didn't want his land overrun by gold-seekers. But when the workers started using gold nuggets to pay for their purchases at a nearby trading post, word got out. By the summer of 1848, the population of gold miners near Sutter's Mill had jumped from just a few hundred to four thousand.

RICH MAN, POOR MAN

John Sutter, owner of Sutter's Mill, where gold was first discovered, must have become rich during the Gold Rush, right? Wrong! The miners he hired looted most of what they found. Then huge crowds set up camp on Sutter's property and stole his sheep and cattle to sell to other squatters for food.

Sutter tried to make money selling supplies and land to the miners, but his agents cheated him and he went bankrupt. Even James Marshall, who had plucked that first gold nugget out of the river, was forced off his land by the prospectors and died penniless.

James Marshall in front of Sutter's Mill, where he first discovered gold.

Gold nuggets, flakes, and even dust were mined during California's gold rush.

"There's Gold in Them Thar Hills!"

Newspapers soon picked up the story of the incredible discovery of gold, and word began to spread even farther. By the fall of 1849, it seemed as if everyone in the world knew that gold had been found in California. The promise of fabulous riches drew thousands to the state from many countries. Because so many came to the gold mines in 1849, they became known as Forty-Niners.

At first, the gold nuggets could simply be picked up off the ground—even by chickens! "Chickens were persistent gatherers of small nuggets of gold," wrote one Forty-Niner, "and their gizzards were regularly searched by the cooks who prepared them for the oven. At Diamond Springs one was killed for a Sunday dinner whose gizzard panned out at $12.80." That's almost $400 in today's money!

Hundreds of Ships from Around the World

Some of the fortune hunters came to California overland across the United States. The journey took many months, and thousands died along the way of disease or starvation.

But most of the gold-seekers traveled to California by ship. In 1849 alone, at least 800 ships docked in San Francisco, the closest port to Sutter's Mill. Many sailed south through the Atlantic Ocean

Gold-seekers who sailed to San Francisco were known as Argonauts.

to Panama, where they hired Natives in dugout canoes to paddle them west. When the river stopped, the travelers mounted horses or mules and rode the rest of the way to the Pacific Ocean. Once the travelers reached the west coast, they had to catch a ship heading north to San Francisco.

Lured by the promise of wealth beyond their wildest dreams, others endured the trip around Cape Horn at the southern tip of South America, braving sudden storms and gale-force winds. Eventually, hundreds of ships completed the treacherous voyage and arrived in San Francisco.

But most of them would never depart.

JUST THE FACTS
Not So Shipshape

No one was surprised when the travelers jumped off the ships as quickly as possible to make their way to the goldfields to strike it rich. But it wasn't just the passengers who left the ships. The crews also often caught the "goldbug" and deserted. Captains couldn't hire anyone to replace them—no one wanted to board a ship and sail away when there was so much gold just waiting to be found.

As soon as most crews caught a glimpse of San Francisco, they jumped ship.

By 1850, San Francisco's harbor was choked with hundreds of abandoned ships.

Miners were amazed to see a woman on the gold fields.

FEMALE FORTY-NINERS

Most of the gold-seekers were men, but there were a few brave women who traveled to California in the 1850s. Many accompanied their husbands, fathers, or brothers. And once they arrived, they could charge high prices for tasks such cooking, mending, doing laundry, and other services that men thought were women's work. Some also worked in saloons or ran boardinghouses.

How few women were there in California's gold-fields? One miner wrote: "Got nearer to a woman this evening than I have been in six months. Came near fainting."

No matter how the captains raged or begged there were no crews to hire. And without sailors, the ships couldn't leave San Francisco. So they sat in the harbor. And sat. The captains despaired as they watched the rugged ships that had so bravely carried them over the rough seas now sitting empty and useless.

The abandoned ships clogged the harbor. Then they began to rot. Ship owners tore out their hair as their expensive vessels became more and more worthless. Some were sold for next to nothing, then dragged onto the beach.

The ships' proud histories meant nothing to the entrepreneurs who cut off masts and top decks and turned the mutilated ships into restaurants, saloons, stores, or warehouses. One ship was used for storing freshwater. Other ships were hardly recognizable as they became hotels, offices, stores, and even a jail.

It got worse. Low-rent apartment houses were built on the decks of other ships—the lower decks became the basements. New owners towed some abandoned ships to what were called ship-breaking yards, where workers ripped them apart and sold their metal fittings and timbers.

Up in Flames

People in San Francisco were desperate for housing and office space, so builders quickly put up structures without proper fireproofing. Many buildings in the city were little more than firetraps. It was no surprise when flames swept through the streets. As more wood was needed for rebuilding, people scavenged timbers and lumbers from the abandoned ships. Some people even burned the once mighty vessels for firewood.

Rotten Row

By 1851, builders had extended San Francisco's wharves and docks out into the harbor as they tried to find more space for the city's exploding population. It wasn't long before buildings were constructed on pilings at the water's edge. As more people flocked to the city, the gold-rush ships were buried under landfill to increase the land available for building in the boomtown. The ships were buried, both in landfill and in people's memories.

The stretch where the ships lay in the sand oozing mud became known as Rotten Row, thanks to the ships' rotting timbers. In just a few decades the ships were landlocked—totally surrounded by regular brick buildings. It was hard to believe they had once sailed the ocean.

HIDDEN

The Buried Ships Are Forgotten ...

Decades went by and the buried ships were completely forgotten. Then, in the 1870s, a building near San Francisco's waterfront was torn down and a new foundation dug. People were amazed at what lay underneath their city: weathered wood that many thought looked like an old floor—but archaeologists realized it was actually the remnants of those once-great ships!

New construction work in San Francisco is still uncovering these ships. When a "carcass" (the body of an old ship) is discovered, work on the building site has to stop immediately. Instead of construction workers using huge diggers and large construction equipment for excavation, archaeologists and historians take over the site armed with brushes, small picks, and other archaeological tools to gently remove layers of dirt. The ship is then slowly and carefully uncovered so it can be identified, cataloged, and possibly moved to a museum.

Experts have been able to name many of the buried ships that have been discovered. If most of the hull is found, they can make a

NEW LAND OUT OF OLD JUNK

San Francisco isn't the only city whose growing population forced the residents to build out into the water. Portland, Maine, has added more than a block of landfill out into the water.

In Toronto, Canada, fishing boats used to sail right up to the back of a large market and unload their catch. Today, thanks to landfill, that market is about 1 kilometer (1.6 miles) from the waterfront.

What's special about San Francisco's landfill is that it was partly made out of amazing, huge ships from all over the world.

Workers were surprised to find ship timbers buried under landfill in downtown San Francisco.

TUNNELS TO KIDNAP SAILORS!

In the 1850s, tunnels were built below the streets of Portland, Oregon. This network connected hotels and bars with the waterfront. Goods moved quickly through the underground passages, avoiding the traffic above.

But it wasn't long before something else was being moved along these tunnels: kidnapped men. They dropped down through trapdoors in bars, then were knocked out by thugs. When they awoke, they were far out at sea, usually headed for China. The men provided cheap labor and were forced to work on the ships with little to eat and terrible living conditions.

good estimate of the ship's length and match it to the records of ships known to have been in San Francisco's harbor. Or archaeologists carefully catalog any damage and repairs they observe, and then look for similar descriptions in records about the ships. Guns, books, and other artifacts found around the hull can also help with identification.

The NIANTIC: From Mighty Ship to a Bit of Rubble

The *Niantic* is probably San Francisco's most famous buried ship. In 1849, it was one of the first ships to arrive bringing eager fortune seekers to the city, having sailed up the west coast from Panama carrying almost 250 gold miners. But as on so many other ships, the entire crew abandoned the ship the moment it reached San Francisco's harbor. An entrepreneur bought the empty vessel for a bargain-basement price when the owner sadly realized he

At one point, the *Niantic* (shown above under
the large flag) was a famous hotel.

would never be able to find a crew to sail the *Niantic* again.

Quickly, the sharp businessman hauled the *Niantic* inland before the original owner could change his mind. The new owner knew storage space around the harbor was in short supply. And anything in short supply was worth a lot of money, he shrewdly figured. He hoped the *Niantic* would turn out to be his gold mine.

Storage was so scarce in the fast-growing city that people paid a whopping $20,000 per month to use the *Niantic*. That was a fortune in those days, worth about $580,000 in today's dollars. But miners were making and losing fortunes almost daily back then, so no one blinked an eye at the exorbitant charge. At one point, the owner cut a doorway right into the side of the *Niantic* so people could easily enter the grounded ship.

Unfortunately, in 1851 the top deck was burned in one of San Francisco's many fires. The once proud *Niantic* now

THE GREAT SHIP NIANTIC

The ship *Niantic* was built in Connecticut in 1832 to carry trade goods to China. In 1844, it became a whaling ship, and five years later a passenger ship.

On July 5, 1849, the *Niantic* arrived in San Francisco with its load of gold miners. Five crew members deserted ship that day, followed by more and more. By July 11 there were only about five left to finish unloading the whole ship. The ship's log ends the very next day. The *Niantic* would never sail the high seas again.

Gold mining could be dangerous, so many Forty-Niners, like this one, carried a knife and pistol.

just looked like a big flat tray floating in the mud. Land was filled in around the old hull and the *Niantic* Hotel was built on it. As other fires ravaged the city, the hotel was rebuilt each time. With every reconstruction it looked less and less like a ship, but in 1852 it was known as the top hotel in San Francisco.

This ship was one of the farthest inland. Likely because of that people talked about it and made many drawings of it, although the hull of the *Niantic* was eventually buried and forgotten. In 1872, it was rediscovered when the hotel was demolished, but the hull was buried yet again during new construction. Then the city's great earthquake of 1906 brought the *Niantic* up out of its subterranean resting place once more. However, the remains of the ship were left in the ground and buried yet again when the street was reconstructed.

The hull remained undisturbed for about 70 years, until excavation for an office complex uncovered it again. Some of its timbers went to a museum and a small portion of the ship was left in the ground. Today, San Francisco's Transamerica Pyramid skyscraper stands beside the last resting place of the *Niantic*, and a nearby plaque tells the story of the mighty ship.

HOW THE GOLD RUSH CHANGED THE WORLD

San Francisco's now buried ships brought about 300,000 gold-seekers to California. The city's population went from 1,000 in 1848 to 25,000 by the end of 1849.

California's Gold Rush has been called the world's first large-scale gold rush. It led to many more gold rushes, in places like Alaska, Australia, Canada, South Africa, and other locations. As in California, it was the early prospectors who made money, while the latecomers went broke. But that didn't stop miners from dreaming of fortunes.

THE SECRET REVEALED
Ride the Subway Right Through an Old Ship!

Other ships buried in San Francisco Bay had names like *Almandralina*, *Balance*, *Candace*, *Euphemia*, and *General Harrison*. Some of the artifacts found deep underground alongside the ships were amazing: jars of olives and gooseberries that were 150 years old but incredibly well preserved, as well as rice bowls and a toy teapot.

When San Francisco's subway was built in the 1960s, many more ship remains were dug up. While some were removed, others had to be left in place so the ground around them wouldn't be further destabilized. When fans head out on the train to the ballpark where the San Francisco Giants play, they likely have home runs and sluggers on their minds, not ancient underground boats. They might be very surprised to find out they're roaring right through the hull of an abandoned and buried gold-rush ship!

"Shiver Me Timbers!"

It's hard to believe that a city as large and world-class as San Francisco is built on buried rotted ships, but more than 40 abandoned ships are known to lie beneath the downtown area—and there may be as many 75. The ships' timbers make the landfill unstable, which is one reason why San Francisco is often greatly damaged by earthquakes.

NUCLEAR RELICS

San Francisco has more underground secrets! Buried in the hills north of the city is an almost forgotten nuclear bunker from the Cold War (see page 66). It was one of the largest ammunition depots on America's west coast, but it became outdated and was almost abandoned.

When it was operational (from 1954 to 1975), this battery would have been heavily guarded, since it was armed with nuclear missiles. They were stored underground, but if enemy planes were detected, the missiles could be elevated to the surface, and computers would guide them into the air.

Today, tourists can descend into the bunker and even watch the missiles—with the nuclear warheads removed, of course!—rise into launch position.

These timbers were found where a ship-breaking yard once stood.

UNDERGROUND DOWNTOWN: SEATTLE

Seattle, Washington, is another west coast American port with underground secrets. The Great Seattle Fire of 1889 destroyed many blocks of the downtown. Since the area often flooded, city leaders decided to rebuild the streets one to two stories higher than the original level.

The old ground floors became the new basements. That lower level of the downtown core was closed in 1907 and mostly forgotten, but about 60 years later a portion of the Seattle Underground was restored and is now open for tours of the abandoned sunken storefronts, forgotten lobbies, and display windows.

However, removing those subterranean wooden hulls and lumber would be even more likely to make the land around them collapse. Without the timbers shoring up the landfill, building foundations would crack, pavement would twist, and landmarks that have stood for decades could topple.

Ask most San Franciscans about the abandoned ships lurking far below their feet and they'll laugh in disbelief. But there are traces if you know where to look. Plaques on skyscraper walls, names embedded in the sidewalks, and even a display in the lobby of a downtown conference center keep the ships from being totally forgotten. That's a good thing, because as San Francisco continues to grow and change, the ships and the city's past will undoubtedly be uncovered again and again.

The General Harrison

The remains of the gold rush supply ship, the General Harrison, lie beneath this building. The sidewalk treatment reminds us that Clay Street was once a wharf at the edge of San Francisco Bay with tidal mud flats to the north, and in 1850 ships like the General Harrison were moored alongside and used as storehouses. The sculpture on the building was inspired by the waterline shape, frames and planking of the ship.

The sidewalk was designed by Topher Delaney and the ship sculpture by Curtis Hollenback and Topher Delaney. They were contributed by Club Quarters™ under the City of San Francisco percent for art program

You can find this plaque near San Francisco's waterfront.

UNDERCOVER SOLDIERS

SOLDIERS

The cave with an explosive secret

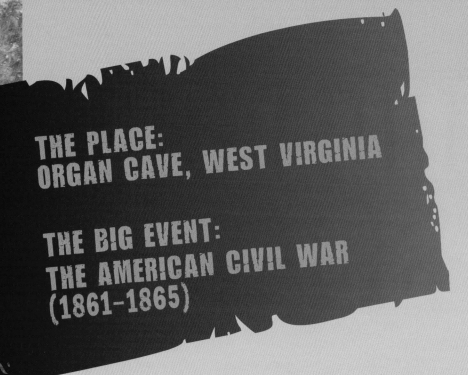

THE PLACE:
ORGAN CAVE, WEST VIRGINIA

THE BIG EVENT:
THE AMERICAN CIVIL WAR
(1861–1865)

"Shhhh!"

The soldier in gray motioned to his fellow soldiers near the mouth of the cave to stop working and stay perfectly still. The Confederate troops instantly froze, their pickaxes and paddles motionless. The men held their breath.

Their lookout had spotted a Union (Northern) soldier—a spy from the opposite side!—furiously searching for any sign of enemy action. Meanwhile, the Confederate (Southern) men in the deep cave below had also received the signal to remain silent and still. If they were discovered, it could mean their deaths, and possible ruin for the entire Confederate Army.

For many long minutes, the Union soldiers searched the nearby trees and looked for enemy footprints in the grass. Finally, the Confederate lookout signaled that the Northern spy had moved on. Quietly, the Southern soldiers got back to work in the tunnels, mining the crucial ingredient for their ammunition.

How could the Union Army not know about the secret hidden right under their feet? Especially a secret that could decide which side would win the war …

THE BEGINNINGS UNCOVERED
Retreat to the Cave!

Confederate General Robert E. Lee surveyed the battleground. And he was not pleased, although his battle with the Union troops at Lewisburg, West Virginia, had started so well. On May 23, 1862, Lee's Southern troops had attacked the Northern army just after dawn. The Confederates took the Union troops by surprise and outnumbered them significantly.

Why were they fighting? America's Northern and Southern states disagreed about many things, including states' rights, how to do business, and, especially, enslavement. Southern states depended on free labor by Black slaves to work their massive plantation fields of such crops as cotton and tobacco. States in the North thought slavery was wrong and had ended it. That made the states in the South worry that they'd be forced to abolish it too. So on April 12, 1861, the two sides began a war that would change America forever.

On this day, more than a year later, the Southern soldiers couldn't keep up with the well-disciplined, fast Northern soldiers. Lee's troops were soon overpowered and on the retreat. They needed a safe place to stop, rest, and eat, and they needed it fast. A place to regroup for another attack, somewhere where they could quickly disappear. But where? They were deep in enemy territory.

Then Lee remembered a huge cave in the area that he'd visited almost 30 years ago. It had lots of space inside, he recalled—perfect for his exhausted troops.

Lee led his soldiers to the cave, and hid them in the trees nearby. He selected a small group of the least tired men to reconnoiter the cave and make sure there were no unpleasant surprises inside, such as concealed Union soldiers. Stealthily, the men crept forward, then disappeared below … into the cave.

The lead soldier held his torch high but it hardly illuminated the deep blackness all around his brave little troop. Carefully, they edged their way down into the cave.

"What was that?" one of the soldiers whispered. Their senses on

Robert Edward Lee, general of the Confederate Army, was a brilliant commander on the battlefield.

The mouth of Organ Cave, which leads into a huge underground room once used for church services, dances, and social events during summer months.

high alert, they stopped instantly, rifles at the ready. Their breathing was loud and ragged, and even the sound of their dripping sweat seemed to echo around the rocky walls.

Tense moments passed. "It's nothing," hissed the leader. "Now let's get moving. Keep your wits about you. The general is counting on us."

The men were still sweating when they finally returned to Lee and the rest of the troop. The group saluted and the leader announced, "All clear."

With a sigh of relief, Lee herded his men down into the subterranean refuge for some much-needed rest.

But it wasn't long before Lee discovered the cave was anything but empty.

JUST THE FACTS

Waterfalls, Ancient Bones, and Red Rivers

The cave Lee and his men camped out in was hundreds of millions of years old. Organ Cave's main entranceway looms about one and a half stories high and its tunnels stretch off in all directions. Even today, no one has mapped them all. Some of the passages are so low that cavers have to squirm through them on their stomachs. As Lee's soldiers would discover, it's easy to get lost in the many passageways.

Organ Cave descends almost 152 meters (500 feet) deep into the ground. Inside is a trio of spectacular waterfalls cascading down more than nine stories. One subterranean river is so rich with iron that its gurgling waters run brilliant red. The splashing and dripping of the water echoes through the cave's rooms, and it surrounded the Southern soldiers with its constant babble.

Here and there, water flows over the cave's rocky walls and floors. As it percolates down, it picks up tiny deposits of chemicals and minerals from the rock. Over millions of years these have pooled in places, forming some of the cave's incredible formations.

One of these looks like a pipe organ, and that's how Organ Cave got its name. Some of the "pipes" are long and some are short, just like in a real organ. Some are narrow and others are wide, again similar to an actual organ. People aren't allowed to touch them now, but visitors used to hit the pipes to hear the different tones they'd make.

There are even "flowers" deep down in Organ Cave. But these flowers are made of the mineral gypsum, which crystallizes out of the cave's water. The gypsum creates curly masses of crystals that look like long, strange flower petals.

The water deep in Organ Cave has attracted many animals over the millions of years. Scientists know from the fossilized bones found here that the cave has sheltered animals ranging from saber-toothed cats and grizzly bears to reindeer and Ice Age porcupines. Thomas Jefferson, America's third president, was very interested in fossils, and in 1796 he was given the fossilized bones of a long-clawed, long-extinct giant ground sloth. Some people in the area believe these bones were found in Organ Cave.

The Jefferson ground sloth used its broad, strong tail for balance when it stretched up.

THAT GIANT GROUND SLOTH

Whatever cave Thomas Jefferson's giant ground sloth came from, it's an incredible find. This type of ground sloth lived as many as 200,000 years ago and was about 3 meters (10 feet) long. It weighed approximately 454 kilograms (1,000 pounds), or about as much as a cow.

Today, you can see the bones that once belonged to Jefferson at the Academy of Natural Sciences in Philadelphia, Pennsylvania. Jefferson's ground sloth is West Virginia's state fossil.

Eight types of bats live in Organ Cave, including this Big Brown Bat.

DANGEROUS DROPPINGS

How did the saltpeter get inside Organ Cave? It's thanks to the bats that live there. You might say they just, er, dropped it there.

Bat droppings, or guano, are full of nitrates, including potassium nitrate, which is also known as saltpeter. Guano is found on the walls and floor of any cave that hosts a colony of bats. Thanks to its high phosphorus and nitrogen content, guano is also a great fertilizer, and for some tiny cave dwellers, it's their only food.

HIDDEN

The Caves Have What the South Needs

But it wasn't the animals and incredible formations that surprised General Robert E. Lee in this secret, underground cavern. Lee noticed that the walls and floor of the cave glittered in the flickering lantern light. The Confederates realized the cave was full of potassium nitrate, or saltpeter.

Saltpeter is the main ingredient in black powder, used to make gunpowder for guns, rifles, cannons, and other weapons. Lee knew Confederate troops desperately needed saltpeter for their ammunition. And now he and his men had stumbled on a limitless source. Suddenly Lee felt his troops were a big step closer to winning the war. But extracting the saltpeter from the cave wouldn't be easy.

Soldiers Digging Deep in the Caves

Making daring raids across the Northern lines, Lee and his soldiers managed to smuggle pickaxes and wooden paddles into Organ Cave. Striking the cave's walls, the blows echoing in the dim light, the soldiers dug the saltpeter-filled rocks and soil out of the floors and walls.

Another group of soldiers, their faces black with dust, shoveled the piles of cave dirt into big cloth bags. Grunting, other soldiers hoisted the bags onto their shoulders and began the treacherous journey farther into the cave. The dim torchlight and uneven rocky trail made the trek dangerous. A stumble could send a man hurtling down into the darkness, to a bottom he couldn't even see.

Sweat poured off the men's faces as they inched their way along steep ledges and crept over the narrow edges of underground cliffs. None of the soldiers dared sing or whistle to relieve the tedium in case the high-pitched sound carried to the entrance of the cave and revealed their hideaway.

Deep in the cave was the men's destination: a large subterranean hall called the hopper room. It was named for the hoppers,

This is one of the hoppers, or saltpeter vats, found years later in Organ Cave.

large V-shaped vats made of wood and lined with straw, that the soldiers had built to refine the cave dirt.

Dirt + Water + Ash

First, the heavy bags of dirt were dumped into the hoppers. Next, the men poured buckets full of water from the cave's rivers over the dirt. The water slowly filtered through the moldy straw, gradually leaching the saltpeter out of the dirt. At the bottom of the hopper was a spout for the water to drain out, down into a trough.

The next group of soldiers scooped the dirty water out of the trough and into huge cast-iron kettles. Here, the men boiled the solution to extract the minerals. Perspiration drenched their clothes as they stirred without ceasing. They also had to add wood ash (from their cooking fires) to transform the mineral from calcium nitrate to potassium nitrate.

When the water finally boiled off, only the white potassium nitrate crystals were left in the bottom of the kettles. These crystals were then bagged, carried up out of Organ Cave, and covertly shipped to factories where the potassium

PETER MONKEYS

Mining the saltpeter was hard work. The workers, called "peter monkeys," dug and shoveled in the icy dark. The logs to make the hoppers and to fuel the fires had to be carried deep into the cave, and so did the water for the process.

The peter monkeys in Organ Cave were able to produce about 75 percent of all the saltpeter the Confederates needed throughout the Civil War. Organ Cave became known as "Lee's Underground Ammo Factory."

Saltpeter is still mined today—though not at Organ Cave—but synthetic saltpeter is now usually used in gunpowder. Currently, saltpeter is added to plant fertilizers, to some foods (such as corned beef) to preserve them, and to soups and stews to thicken them. It's also becoming well known as an important ingredient in toothpaste for sensitive teeth.

TUNNEL WARFARE

Organ Cave isn't the only underground location important in the Civil War. In June 1864, Union soldiers began digging a tunnel in Petersburg, Virginia. The idea was to create a passage under the Confederate Army, fill it with explosives, and blow a hole in the Southern army's defenses.

Early on July 30, 1864, the tunnel was completed and the fuse on the blast was lit. You can still see the crater the explosion created; the conflict became known as the Battle of the Crater. However, the Union soldiers who led the charge after the blast weren't properly trained. There was such confusion that the Confederates won the battle.

Union soldiers placing explosives in a tunnel under enemy Confederate lines before the Battle of the Crater.

nitrate was mixed with sulfur and charcoal to make gunpowder for Southern guns.

It was dirty, exhausting work in the still air so deep underground, but the soldiers knew how important it was to keep their side supplied with ammunition. The mining and extraction was stressful too, because the men worried they'd be discovered by the nearby Northerners at any moment.

Southern Soldiers Keep Disappearing!

From time to time, Union troops were shocked to spot Southern soldiers around Organ Cave. The Northerners would race after the Confederate troops to tackle them for questioning, but the Confederates would disappear. The Northerners scratched their heads—it was as if the ground had just swallowed up the Southerners.

The Union soldiers didn't know that Organ Cave had 11 different entrances. The Southerners could quickly slip into any one of them and be gone in an instant. Sometimes there would be Union soldiers camping directly overhead while the Confederate troops toiled away right below them. The Northerners knew nothing about what was going on just beneath their feet.

Confederate officials sometimes even held Sunday church services in their hiding spot. Organ Cave is so large that more than 1,000 soldiers could fit under the shelter of the cave's huge underground entrance. The excellent natural acoustics meant that sound carried well to even the farthest worshipper.

THE SECRET REVEALED

End of the Battle: Leaving the Cave Behind

The Confederate troops abandoned Organ Cave in early November 1863 when they were ordered out to fight in the Battle of Droop Mountain nearby. There were more than four times as many Union soldiers as Confederate, and the Southerners lost badly. The few survivors never returned to Organ Cave. The Union Army only discovered the Confederates' underground secret after the Civil War was over.

The Civil War ended on April 9, 1865, when General Lee surrendered to the Union forces. The Confederate states were in ruins and it took decades for them to recover.

Teenagers Discover Organ Cave

For many years after the Civil War no one who lived around Organ Cave knew the important role it had played during the conflict. The secret was buried deep underground.

Then one day some teenagers found their way into the cave. They explored the many tunnels and scrambled far

WARTIME CAVE

Organ Cave has a long military history. During the American Revolution in the late 1700s, people hid valuables in it. During the War of 1812, experts think soldiers may have already begun mining saltpeter out of the cave.

Later, during the Cold War (page 66), the United States government believed Organ Cave could make a good shelter from nuclear fallout. The cave was filled with crackers and dehydrated food, as well as medications and water. There were enough supplies for 500 people to live there for about two weeks. However, Organ Cave was never actually used as a shelter.

Confederate soldiers and other people scratched messages onto the rocks of Organ Cave.

Organ Cave's stalagmites and stalactites are still growing.

HANGING AROUND

Organ Cave is classified as an active cave. That means its formations keep growing, thanks to the water and minerals running over them. The *stalagmites* and *stalactites* in Organ Cave keep lengthening.

Stalactites are icicle-like formations that hang from a cave's ceiling. They form when calcium carbonate (also the main ingredient in eggshells) drips down. *Stalagmites* are made of the same chemical but form on a cave's floor and grow up.

deeper into the cave than anyone had been for decades. Their flashlights lit up the underground rivers and strange formations that had sat in silence and utter darkness for so long. Deep down in the depths the teens discovered a huge room, scattered with strange shapes built from old wood.

At first, the decrepit wooden frames looked like ancient junk. But when the teenagers crawled out of Organ Cave and told others about their incredible find, experts returned to the cave to take a closer look.

People were amazed to realize the wood structures were hoppers and that they dated back to

Saber-toothed cat fossils like this one were found deep in Organ Cave.

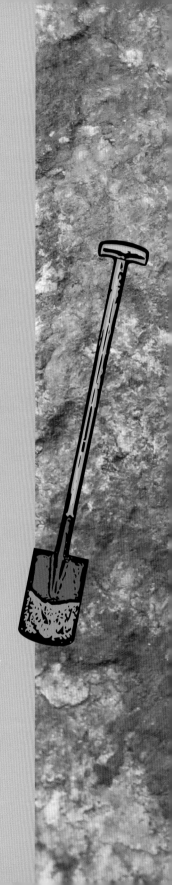

Civil War times. The tallies the soldiers had left on the walls and the lists they'd scratched into the rock told more of the story.

Dog Room and Straddle Alley

Organ Cave has as many as 113 kilometers (70 miles) of carefully mapped cave passages. That number keeps increasing as cavers explore more and more of the dark tunnels winding their way into the mountain. There are areas with names such as Blowhole, Dog Room, Sally's Waterfall, Straddle Alley, and Throne Room. The names are based on the rocks and formations found in Organ Cave.

The saber-toothed cats and reindeer are long gone from the cave, but there are still animals there, ranging from bats and salamanders to slime molds. Thanks to the water in Organ Cave, cavers also find fish and insects. These animals live deep in the cave where the sun's light can't reach. Since they have no need for eyes, over many years they've lost the ability to see.

UNDERGROUND ATLANTA

During the Civil War, Atlanta, Georgia, was burned to the ground by the Union Army. The city was rebuilt to accommodate trains, so raised roadways, or viaducts, were added. Store owners began to move their storefronts up a story to the level of the new roads.

During Prohibition (page 40) some of the rooms in the basements were used as speakeasies (illegal saloons). Over the next 40 years, this lower level was abandoned and forgotten. Then, in the late 1960s, the area was rediscovered and today "Underground Atlanta" is full of shops and restaurants.

DESTRUCTION OF THE DEPOTS, PUBLIC BUILDINGS, AND MANUFACTORIES AT ATLANTA, GEORGIA, November 15, 1864.

THE FOURTEENTH AND TWENTIETH CORPS MOVING OUT OF ATLANTA, November 15, 1864.

On November 15, 1864, William Sherman, general of the Union Army, ordered the destruction of most of Atlanta's buildings.

The Answer Was Underground!

The Civil War was America's deadliest war ever. By the end of it, about 750,000 soldiers from both armies were dead, and many civilians had died and been injured as well.

For many years, no one could figure out how the Southerners were able to get enough gunpowder to keep fighting, since the North had cut off many of its enemy's supply lines. Finding the hoppers far underground inside Organ Cave solved the mystery. Perhaps Organ Cave has many more answers—and surprises—deep in its tunnels and passages.

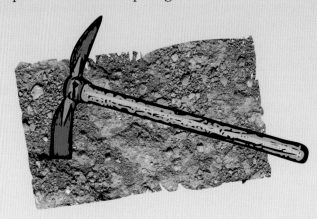

GANGSTERS BELOW-GROUND

The little place on the prairie that became a crime hub

THE PLACE:
MOOSE JAW, SASKATCHEWAN, CANADA

THE BIG EVENT:
PROHIBITION (1918–1933)

Scritch, scritch, scritch! Rats scrambled through the pitch-black damp of the silent tunnels. Along the low passageways, tiny subterranean insects with too many legs scuttled over the packed-earth ceilings, sometimes trapping themselves in the thick cobwebs.

The foul smell of mold made the air hard to breath. When a heavy truck rumbled through the streets of Moose Jaw above, the wooden supports groaned and little showers of dirt fell to the floor of the tunnels.

At one time, people worked and even lived in these passages. The lamps they used to light their secret—often illegal—activities now hung empty and dark. After the criminals and others left, decades passed as the tunnels waited, empty and forgotten.

But the people would be back. Someone always returned.

THE BEGINNINGS UNCOVERED

Going Underground to Escape Winter Wind

Moose Jaw is a bustling city in south-central Saskatchewan. Under vast prairie skies and surrounded by endless wheat fields, the city is an important terminal on the cross-Canada railroad. Farmers depend on it to ship their crops east and west across the country, as well as south into the United States. Moose Jaw looks like many other normal prairie towns—not like a city with a secret buried deep beneath it.

Back in the early 1900s, most of Moose Jaw's larger buildings were heated by boilers in their basements. The boilers produced steam to warm the offices and shops above. This was cutting-edge technology for the time. In the winter, Moose Jaw's buildings needed lots of heat. Frigid western winds blew through the city streets, dropping the temperatures well below freezing.

Engineers who looked after the heating systems hated going out in the bitter cold as they moved from building to building. Brrr! So they quickly came up with a brilliant solution. The engineers dug a series of tunnels linking the warm basements.

The tunnels extended for blocks in many directions. Most had rough dirt walls, though some were lined with stones or timber. A few lights hanging from the ceiling lit the way—and made the cobwebs in the dim corners easy to overlook.

No matter how bitter the winds or how much snow fell, the staff stayed toasty underground while they moved equipment around and kept the furnaces going. How could the engineers know they would be only the first of many groups to travel through the gloomy, dirt-packed passageways below the city's streets?

The Railway Comes to Town

Moose Jaw was a young, booming city in those days. It was founded in 1882 when the Canadian Pacific Railway was being

CANADA

●←——Moose Jaw

UNITED STATES

MOOSE JAW

How does a town get a name like Moose Jaw? Some people think it comes from Plains Cree words meaning "a warm place by the river" or "warm breezes." Others say that Moose Jaw River looks like a moose's jaw.

The Snowbirds, Canada's top flight-demonstration team, are based here. The city is also known for the giant murals showing its history. If you're a Harry Potter fan, you probably already know the city is "home" to the Moose Jaw Meteorites, one of the world's best Quidditch teams!

built to link far-flung cities across the vast country. Officials located a town at the site because it was a convenient place to cross the Moose Jaw River, which provided the railway with a good water supply. That was important for fueling the steam locomotives of the time.

Rail travel was important in the United States as well. A cross-country railroad had been completed there in 1869. In 1903, Moose Jaw was linked to a rail line heading north from Chicago, an important hub on the American railroad system. In less than two decades, some rather unsavory characters would make use of that connection—and of Moose Jaw's buried tunnels. But before that, the city's hidden passageways would find another use.

Workers Hide from Racism—Below the Streets

To build the railway across Canada, many workers had been brought to British Columbia, on the Pacific coast, from China. They worked hard but were often paid as little as half of what other workers earned. That was very unfair, but because the immigrant workers accepted the lower wages, they were hired quickly.

Some Canadian and European rail workers became angry; they felt the Chinese men were taking their jobs. The Asian immigrants were often threatened or beaten up.

Chinese laborers hard at work on the Canadian Pacific Railway in British Columbia in 1884.

The situation got worse. By the early 1880s about 15,000 workers had come to Canada from China and started to spread across the country. The Canadian government became concerned about having so many immigrants from one nation living in the country. They decided to charge Chinese people a fee if they wanted to move to Canada.

In 1885, this fee, or head tax, was $50, but by 1903 it had increased to $500. At the time, it took Chinese workers about two years to make that much money. It was almost impossible for the rail workers to pay the tax. The fee was especially discriminatory because Chinese people were the only immigrants who had to pay a tax to enter Canada.

The Chinese men couldn't escape across the border to the United States. There, Chinese laborers had been barred from entering the country in 1882, and immigration of all Chinese people was banned in 1888. But it was clear the Chinese workers weren't wanted in Canada either. They needed to quickly find a way to escape not only the beatings, but also the impossibly high head tax. They couldn't afford to go home to China, so those who lived in Moose Jaw decided to go underground—literally!

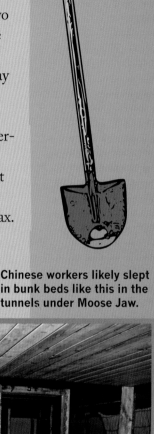

Chinese workers likely slept in bunk beds like this in the tunnels under Moose Jaw.

Tunnel Dwellers

The Chinese men slipped away into the network of tunnels below the city that the engineers had dug years earlier. The technicians rarely used the tunnels anymore, so they were almost abandoned. Most people in Moose Jaw had no idea where the Chinese workers had gone.

Many of the immigrants had friends who'd paid the head tax and were in Canada legally. These men ran restaurants and laundries at street level, and provided their

illegal countrymen with work, food, and other supplies. And many of those businesses were connected to the secret underground passageways.

Trapdoors, hidden hatches, and concealed entrances in the street-level businesses gave the below-surface dwellers access to the rest of the world—but only when no one else was looking. There were few chances to visit with legal friends or relatives, or slip out for a breath of fresh air.

The smell of sweat and fear hung heavily in the thick, dank air. All day long, the men had to sit quietly in the murky, damp tunnels so no one in the shops and restaurants above would suspect they were there. Only at night could they move about without fear of discovery.

Meals were held around long worn tables, with the men sitting on rickety chairs and packed in shoulder to shoulder. Their narrow bunk beds were crammed together in one darker section of the tunnels. With its rough floors, earthen walls, and rat-infested passages, the men's home was more like a prison.

Some Chinese men lived in the dark, claustrophobic tunnels for years. They rarely saw the sun or caught even a glimpse of the sky. Dim lanterns provided the only light in their lives.

Many of the men couldn't afford to bring their wives and children from China to join them. They spent their sad, lonely days with other men who could no longer safely work above ground but couldn't afford to leave a country that didn't want them. The men could only lie on their thin, narrow beds, wistfully dreaming of the lives and families they'd left behind.

A few of the men convinced women to marry them and share their bleak, subterranean existence. Couples even raised children in the dark network below Moose Jaw. The children played in the tunnels, running up and down the narrow passageways, ducking into shadowy corners for hide-and-seek.

There were no school classrooms for these kids—the adults taught them as best they could wherever they could find space. At least the tunnels were fairly warm in the freezing winters, since the passageways were close to heated basements.

Soon the Chinese families had company in those tunnels. Very dangerous company …

JUST THE FACTS
The Trouble with Alcohol

In the last half of the 1800s, many North Americans saw alcohol as a big problem. Drinkers, mostly men, gulped away much of their money (often the family's only money, since few women could work for pay in those days) in bars. Meanwhile, their wives and children starved. There was no welfare system to provide for families left penniless by all of this drinking.

It seemed drunkenness and misery were everywhere. But as women began to get the right to vote and gain more power in society, they demanded change. Many people, especially women, thought getting rid of liquor would be a good start.

So governments decided to prohibit the making, transport, and sale of alcohol. By 1918, Prohibition was in force in Canada, and two years later it was the law in the United States.

Prohibition's Surprising Effects

Some people resented having someone else tell them what they could and couldn't drink. Others, especially those with money, figured they could "buy" their way around the law. People in power might publicly speak out against alcohol, but when no one was looking, it was a different story.

Posters such as this one from the Women's Christian Temperance Union (W.C.T.U.) encouraged people to support Prohibition.

Plebiscite Series—No. 5.

THE SALOON MUST GO.

THE saloon must go, or law will go.

THE saloon lives by law, and by law it must die.

VICE is to be prohibited, let the difficulties in executing the law be what they may.—*Lord Chesterfield.*

THE saloon is the high-school of high crimes and misdemeanors.

THE school-room is ennobling; the bar-room is ignobling.

NOTHING noble is born of the liquor traffic.—*John G. Holland.*

PULVERIZE the rum power and you empty prisons and police-stations.

UNDER the malign influence of the saloon in municipal affairs demagogues leap into power, and subordinate public good to the management of the criminal classes.

SALOON-RULE in large cities is making government a farce and a failure.

AS THE saloon in politics outlaws moral men, will not moral men outlaw the saloon?

THE CASE STATED.—The argument for No License may be concisely stated in four propositions:

1. The business interests of our country demand the suppression of their worst foe—the saloon.

2. The interests of Canadian homes demand the suppression of their worst foe—the saloon.

3. The political liberty of our country demands the suppression of its worst foe—the saloon.

4. The conscience of the country demands that the attitude of government toward the foe of business, home, and liberty should be one of uncompromising hostility.

THE day is coming when the Canadian people will look back to these saloon days as the darkest page in national annals.

VOTE PROHIBITION !

Dominion W.C.T.U. Literature Depository, 56 Elm St., Toronto.

Price, 15 cts. per 100; $1.25 per 1000. Postage, 15 cts. per 1000.

Top politicians and law enforcers often drank in private saloons with their friends. The illegal smuggling of alcohol—by bootleggers (who concealed bottles in their boots or pants) or rumrunners (who carried liquor across rivers or lakes)—skyrocketed, and so did the creation of secret drinking places, known as speakeasies.

People could buy alcohol through government facilities if they could prove they needed it for scientific, religious (such as wine for Communion), and industrial uses (for cleaning and sterilization)—but it was often drunk for very different reasons!

1920s Crime Spree

During Prohibition, some women smuggled liquor in small flasks that they stuck in their garters.

Criminals saw the opportunity Prohibition gave them: people wanted liquor and gangs provided it. Organized crime groups and other gangsters took control of the distribution of alcohol. There was lots of money to be made, so gangs guarded their territories brutally. Fear held cities in its grip as gunshots rang out on the streets and police sirens blared through the night.

Thanks to Prohibition, crime went wild during the 1920s. Chicago was at the center of it all. Because the city is on the shores of Lake Michigan, alcohol could easily be brought in by boat. It came from countries such as Bermuda and Mexico, or the French islands of Saint-Pierre and Miquelon off Canada's east coast.

The bootleggers' small, speedy boats could outrun government ships across lakes and zoom along narrow, shallow rivers. Chicago was also well connected by railroads to many cities—including Moose Jaw. Liquor could be moved quickly to and from almost anywhere.

A gang called the Chicago Outfit became famous for bootlegging liquor and other crimes. The group soon became known as the Capones, taking the name of their boss, Al Capone, who was one of the world's most notorious American gangsters.

HIDDEN

Meanwhile, Back in Moose Jaw ...

When Prohibition was brought in, Moose Jaw's tunnels got a whole new use. The town was a major railway terminus linked to the U.S., but it was also remote enough that it didn't get a lot of media or police attention. Since it's in Canada, it was beyond the reach of the American police, which was handy for the bootleggers.

Moose Jaw's network of buried tunnels made it especially attractive to criminals. One tunnel supposedly went right under the railway station and opened into a shed in the rail yards. Gangsters could load and unload bottles with no fear of being seen.

Between shipments, liquor was hidden in the tunnels. Crates and barrels lined the passageways, stacked high against the damp walls. Gangs of thugs lived and worked underground, alongside the illegal Chinese workers who still made their home there. The two groups mostly ignored each other and got along fairly well.

Moose Jaw became a capital for distributing illegal liquor in Canada and the United States. Soon Moose Jaw was one of the wildest towns in Canada's West. Most of the gangsters who visited the city came from Chicago, so Moose Jaw earned the nickname Little Chicago.

This tunnel in downtown Tulsa, Oklahoma, connects the Philtower Building and Philcade Building.

TULSA'S TUNNELS

Moose Jaw isn't the only city with Prohibition tunnels. Buried under the streets of Tulsa, Oklahoma, are secret walkways built in 1929 by Waite Phillips, one of the city's top businessmen.

Phillips had heard about the kidnapping and holding for ransom of wealthy entrepreneurs in Chicago during the lawlessness of Prohibition. He felt he and other rich executives in Tulsa could also be in danger. Phillips had tunnels built to link eight skyscrapers, creating secret hiding places and extra exits.

Today, you can see some of the tunnels, but most people in Tulsa have no idea what's hiding below their feet!

PURPLE SKYLIGHTS

In downtown Havre, Montana, there are small purple glass squares in the sidewalk. These are skylights for secret underground passageways dating back more than one hundred years.

The tunnels were built by Chinese immigrants who, like their countrymen in Moose Jaw, were trying to escape violence and persecution aboveground. They eventually moved out, but when fire destroyed Havre's business district in 1904 businesses on the street level moved underground and the skylights were added.

Later, the tunnels were used for illegal activities, including smuggling alcohol during Prohibition. As years passed, the tunnels were forgotten, but in the 1990s they were restored and opened to tourists.

The skylights weren't always purple: the manganese (a metallic element) in the glass reacted with sunlight, turning the skylights mauve.

During Prohibition, police poured liquor they found into sewers to keep people from drinking it.

Some considered the city a gangsters' resort, possibly even frequented by the infamous Capone. Between jobs, the gangsters hung out in the tunnels, careful to stay hidden from the police. The thugs drank and gambled, sometimes resulting in deadly arguments.

Did Capone Hide Out in Moose Jaw?

No photos or written records exist to prove that Capone was ever in Moose Jaw or hid out in its tunnels. But would a slippery crook like Capone leave behind evidence of his whereabouts?

Some Moose Javians believe Capone definitely visited their town and its secret passageways. A local man remembered that as a teen in the 1920s he was often hired to buy Chicago newspapers for one of the town's gangsters. The work seemed fairly innocent until a day when the well-dressed thug told young Ken that his boss wanted to meet him.

At first, Ken refused to accompany the mobster. But,

Al Capone made Chicago one of North America's most lawless cities during Prohibition.

"When the boss wants to see you, you go," the teenager was told.

Ken stumbled into the big man's room, where Capone was encircled by tall, beefy goons, all carrying guns. *What had Ken gotten himself into?*

However, Capone politely introduced himself and thanked Ken for picking up the newspapers. Then he offered Ken some money as a tip. But the teen had been taught never to take money from strangers and he refused. Capone assumed this meant Ken was a sharp negotiator and wanted more money. The gangster offered the boy a bigger bill. Ken still refused.

The bodyguards weren't used to anyone saying no to their boss. One of them reached for his gun! Luckily, Capone told Ken just to leave—and he ran out of there as fast as he could.

There are other stories about a messenger boy seeing Capone in his office deep in the tunnels, surrounded by cases of liquor bottles. Despite the deep shadows and murk, the boy recognized the crime king by the scars on his face. A Moose Jaw barber is said to have

PUBLIC ENEMY NUMBER ONE

There may be no definite proof that crime boss Al Capone was ever in Moose Jaw. But there's no doubt that he is America's most infamous gangster.

Capone's life of crime began in 1913, when he joined a gang at age 14. By 1930, this ruthless killer controlled the bootlegging business from Canada to Florida. Using bribes and intimidation, he manipulated Chicago's judges, police, and politicians.

But eventually Capone's reign of terror came to an end. He spent four years in prison (for tax evasion!) before dying in 1947.

Police uncovered this huge still (a machine for making, or distilling, liquor) in 1922.

"CHEESE IT! IT'S THE HEAT!"

Gangsters in Prohibition times had their own language so they could talk about their illegal schemes without giving away details to other people. If the criminals had to hide because policemen were making life "hot" for them, they might say, "Cheese it! It's the heat!"

If you double-crossed a goon (thug), you might hear some chin music (get a punch on the jaw). Or you could be zotzed (killed) with a roscoe (gun) and end up in a Chicago overcoat (coffin). Of course, if the trouble boy (gangster) got caught, he'd be in bracelets (handcuffs) and under glass (in jail). Savvy? (Get it?)

visited Capone deep in the tunnels a number of times to cut his hair. The man kept quiet about his amazing story—until after he knew Capone was definitely dead.

The End of Prohibition

Prohibition had ended in most of Canada by 1930 and in the United States in 1933. Although many people had thought Prohibition would be a good idea, some experts felt there had never been so much crime in the United States.

With Prohibition over and alcohol available legally again, American rumrunners were out of a job and no longer had to stay concealed in Moose Jaw's dark tunnels. Most moved back to Chicago. By this time many of the Chinese people had left Moose Jaw. As well, the head tax that had forced them into the tunnels was removed in 1923, so they no longer had to hide belowground.

Little by little, everyone moved out of the deep passageways. They became derelict and unsafe. Entrances were boarded up and exits covered over. Eventually, the tunnels were forgotten.

THE SECRET REVEALED

A Great Big Hole in Main Street

For many years, Moose Jaw officials denied there were any tunnels under the city. Perhaps they felt the stories about the tunnels were just tall tales. Or maybe they didn't want anyone to get injured exploring the deteriorating passageways.

Then, according to local folklore, one day in the 1970s people along the city's Main Street got a huge shock. They watched in amazement as part of the pavement collapsed and a car fell through the road. It came to rest in a deep hole. When investigators arrived on the scene, they found there wasn't just one big hole under the streets but a whole network of tunnels. Moose Jaw's secret passageways had finally been brought to light again.

Only a few of the tunnels have been found—based on the stories that are told, there were likely lots more used during

Today, actors like this one in Moose Jaw's tunnels help bring the Prohibition era to life.

Moose Jaw isn't the only city to claim an underground Capone connection. Not surprisingly, in Chicago hidden tunnels connect local bars, and Capone and his goons were said to use them to escape from police raids or from attacks by rival gangs.

In Thornton, Illinois (about 30 minutes from Chicago), a bar Capone owned sat on top of a network of tunnels that were said to be a dumping ground for the bodies of people who got on his bad side. And that wasn't hard to do!

Prohibition. It's thought that many stores and restaurants in Moose Jaw still have entrances to the tunnels, but the doorways are hidden behind forgotten or lost false walls.

Gangsters and Fugitives ... and Tourists

Old bottles and wooden rum-bottle cases left behind in Moose Jaw's subterranean passages revealed their importance to the crime world during Prohibition. Stories passed down through families told how the tunnels sheltered frightened Chinese workers from racism.

Moose Jaw's underground passageways have been restored and are now one of the city's most popular tourist attractions. You can tour them to find out about bootlegging, as well as the Chinese immigration experience.

Actors are there to make characters from both eras come alive. You can hide out from Moose Jaw's police chief with other gangsters, or be a Chinese immigrant slipping through the blackness from one friend's laundry to another friend's café. You never know what might happen when modern times shine a bright light on the dark history of Moose Jaw's incredible tunnels.

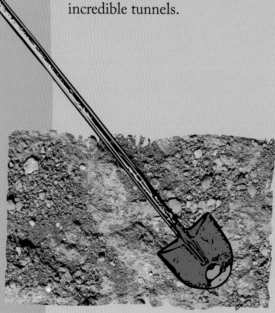

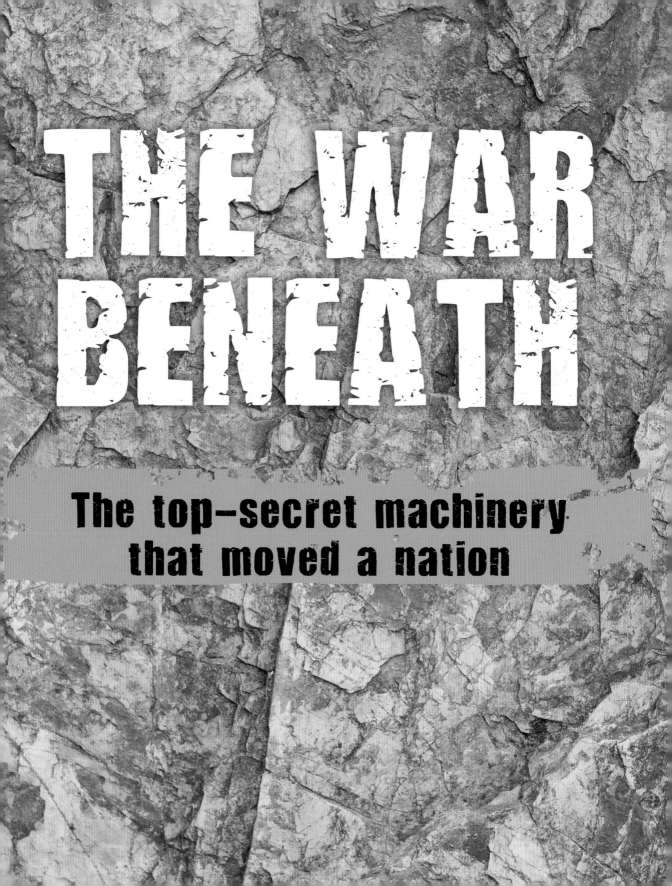

THE WAR BENEATH

The top-secret machinery that moved a nation

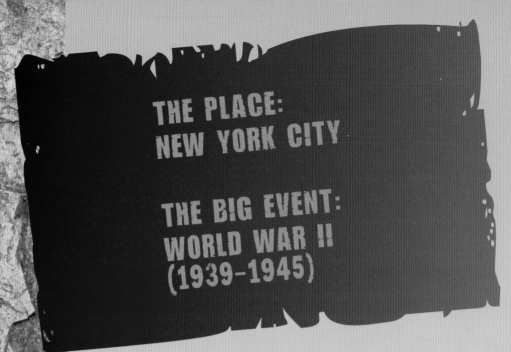

THE PLACE:
NEW YORK CITY

THE BIG EVENT:
WORLD WAR II
(1939–1945)

"Shoot first and ask questions later," ordered the officer. "Understand, soldiers?"

"Sir, yes, sir," barked the two young men.

"And never," thundered the officer, "ever, take your eyes off that elevator door!"

"Sir, yes, sir," repeated the two soldiers, hoisting their rifles to their shoulders and facing the elevator.

During World War II, the world's fate depended on those soldiers guarding vital machinery ten stories below one of the world's largest train terminals. Only certain Americans were even aware the equipment existed, let alone guessed its importance.

The guards had to be constantly vigilant against enemy spies who conspired to destroy the apparatus. Their eyes trained on the elevator doors, the soldiers kept their guns at the ready. If anyone stepped off the elevator who didn't belong there—well, the guards had their orders.

Even today, with the gear's importance long ago mothballed, its exact location is still classified information. Few people are allowed to view this secret sub-basement, ten stories underground.

And believe it or not, that isn't the only incredible secret hidden around this train terminal deep below the sidewalks of New York City.

THE BEGINNINGS UNCOVERED

Spies Land in Maine

Erich Gimpel peered into the icy blackness. Ahead of his tiny rubber raft stretched a beach on the east coast of the United States, a nation at war with his own. Behind the secret agent lurked the sleek black Nazi submarine that had brought him across the ocean.

Back in Europe, on this cold, late-November night in 1944, World War II was going badly for Gimpel's homeland of Germany. A few months earlier, the D-Day invasion had delivered more than 300,000 Allied troops (from America, Britain, Canada, and many other countries) to France. The German army was being beaten in many bloody battles and forced to retreat.

But the Nazis weren't giving up yet. Gimpel and his fellow spy, William Colepaugh (pronounced *COAL-paw*), could perhaps turn everything around if they succeeded in their secret mission. They were to make their way to New York to gather and transmit secret military information, as well as sabotage America's war effort.

Operation Elster

The spies' sabotage had one frightening objective. The German spy network, the Abwehr (pronounced *AB-vare*; it's German for "defense"), had discovered the location of some vital American machinery. This equipment controlled every one of the trains on America's east coast, the launching ground for the ships that carried millions of American soldiers to Europe to fight for the Allies.

If the spies could destroy the machinery that controlled the trains—and therefore the troop

Grand Central Terminal was a busy place during World War II.

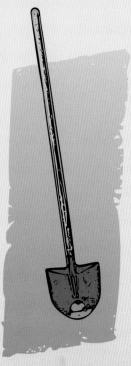

movements—American fighters would be stranded in America, unable to get to Europe to battle the Nazis. If all those troops couldn't join the Allies, Germany would have a chance of winning the war. And Gimpel and Colepaugh knew exactly where that vital mechanism was located: deep below the bustling railroad tracks of New York City's Grand Central Terminal.

Operation Elster—German for "magpie," a bird known for being a thief—had begun.

JUST THE FACTS

A Sabotage Target Under the Subway System

The target of Operation Elster was the secret sub-basement many stories below Grand Central Terminal's train and subway systems. About two stories high, this vast mechanical control room was crammed full of machinery. Pipes and ducts snaked along the walls, while greasy levers and dials kept the equipment humming. The sub-basement was code-named M42—the "42" refers to Grand Central Terminal's location at 42nd Street and Park Avenue in New York.

Converters like this one were the target of the Nazis' Operation Elster.

Hidden deep in M42 were the 12 converters that changed alternating current (AC) to direct current (DC) and supplied the DC traction current to the entire terminal. The converters powered all the trains that passed through, so they were incredibly important and powerful. Disastrously, however, they had one fatal flaw—they were easy to sabotage. They could be completely disabled if an enemy agent dumped something as simple as a bucket of sand on them. The gears would grind to a halt—and so would American troop movement.

No wonder then that during World War II this subterranean equipment room was one of the most closely guarded facilities in the entire United States. At all times, day and night, armed guards kept their eyes—

and guns—trained on the doors to this secret underground control room.

The leaders in the highest level of the American armed forces knew how vital the secret converters were to the war effort. But they were also desperately aware of how easily even a single spy could destroy them, in just seconds.

Ears and Eyes Everywhere

The German Abwehr had spies everywhere, even in the most secure halls of the American defense system. These shadowy men and women were always listening, picking up whispers here, rumors there. They knew that a bribe to a greedy secretary or the threat of torture to a scared soldier would eventually bring them the information they craved.

The Nazi spies pieced together scraps of information and ferreted out the secret of the Grand Central Terminal's vital subterranean power grid. They quickly sent the classified location home by coded message to Germany. Their country's leader, Adolf Hitler, smiled with evil satisfaction as he read the note. Then he ordered the immediate destruction of the converters.

Gimpel and Colepaugh were assigned to carry out the sabotage. All of their Abwehr training had led up to this single moment on the icy Maine beach in November 1944.

Heading to New York

Gimpel felt that to infiltrate American society he needed a partner who not only could speak perfect English with an American accent, but also really knew about life in the United States. The Nazi spy believed his companion should be able to talk about baseball, popular songs, Hollywood gossip, and other everyday American things that often trip up spies.

Since Colepaugh had been born in the U.S., he was a natural for

Adolf Hitler was dictator of Nazi Germany from 1934 to 1945.

the job. He didn't have the same espionage training Gimpel did, but Gimpel felt they'd work well together. However, Gimpel would soon discover he'd have been much better off if he'd shot the American and left him to die on that frozen beach.

Instead, the two spies struggled together through the snow to the road. They carried heavy suitcases and were wearing only light coats that hardly protected them from the weather. When a taxi finally stopped for them, Colepaugh lied and said their car had gone into a ditch. The cabbie drove the pair to a nearby train station. It wasn't long before they arrived at Grand Central Terminal in New York City.

Before the Nazi agents could begin their assault on the secret sub-basement, they needed to find a place to live and set up their radio transmitter. When this was done, Gimpel began trying to gather military information and figure out how to infiltrate M42.

However, Colepaugh decided to enjoy himself in New York. He soon realized espionage wasn't for him. But the reluctant secret agent knew that if he said anything to Gimpel about his change of heart, the German would kill him.

Spy on the Loose

So Colepaugh simply disappeared—but first he packed all the pair's money and guns into a suitcase and took them with him. When Gimpel discovered Colepaugh had abandoned him, he figured the American might have returned to Grand Central Terminal, since that was where the pair had entered New York City.

Gimpel was right, and he also found Colepaugh's suitcase in the baggage storage at the terminal and managed to pick it up, even though he didn't have the claim ticket. Now Gimpel had all the loot. When Colepaugh later returned for the bag and found it gone, he realized Gimpel must have it and that the German had likely figured out his plans. Colepaugh had to think fast.

Erich Gimpel, right front, and William Colepaugh were escorted by police to their trial in 1945.

The American-born spy turned himself in to the FBI (Federal Bureau of Investigation). He did his best to convince the officials that he was a double agent who was actually working for the Allies and that they should let him go and instead arrest Gimpel. The interrogators weren't tricked by Colepaugh but used his information to try to nab Gimpel too. The German eluded capture for a few days, but he was soon arrested. Neither spy had stepped near M42. Thanks to Colepaugh, Operation Elster was over almost before it had begun.

THE DISAPPEARING NIGHTCLUB

New York has an underground Prohibition connection, just like Moose Jaw (page 40). At Club "21," if the doorman saw police arriving to raid the club, he pushed an alarm button. Liquor on tables was whisked away. Behind the bar, the shelves holding the bottles and glasses were tipped backward. Everything fell down a secret shaft directly into the city's sewer system.

The club's liquor was stored in a secret cellar in the basement, behind a door that looked like a brick wall and had a hidden lock. It was never discovered by police during Prohibition.

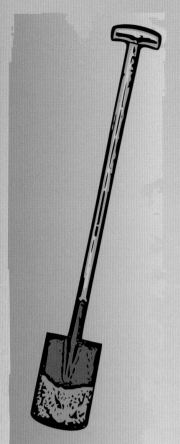

One of only two photos that exist showing
President Franklin Delano Roosevelt in a wheelchair.

HIDDEN

Hiding in Plain Sight

Gimpel and Colepaugh had no idea, but Grand Central Terminal's underground train tunnels hold more secrets. One of the biggest may have involved the American president during World War II, Franklin Delano Roosevelt.

Since 1921, Roosevelt had been barely able to walk, due to polio, a paralyzing disease. He could stand for only a short time and had to lean heavily on canes or helpers. The rest of the time he usually used a wheelchair.

The politician had an agreement with the press at the time that they would never publish photos of him that displayed his disability. Thanks to cell phone cameras and social media sites like Twitter, it's hard to imagine a politician or celebrity getting away with an arrangement like that today.

Why did Roosevelt work so hard to conceal his disability? Back in the 1930s and 1940s, many people didn't think disabled persons could handle demanding jobs. Especially during the dark years of World War II, it was important for the American people to have complete faith in their president. Roosevelt knew the only way this would be possible was if most Americans had no idea how disabled he was.

It was especially hard for Roosevelt to hide his condition when he boarded or exited trains. Since he could do neither by himself, he had to rely on aides to lift him out of or into a waiting railcar. Unless there was another way, perhaps with the help of a gloomy, all-concealing secret tunnel …

The Secret Underground Railcar

That's where the strange railcar still rusting away deep below New York's elegant Waldorf Astoria hotel may have come in. Unlike a regular railcar, this one is large enough and strong enough to hold a full-size automobile. It's armor-clad, with bulletproof glass. Some

It's hard to believe this rusty old railcar may once have carried a president— or two.

DEEP DOWN CHICAGO

New York City isn't the only big American city with abandoned train secrets far below the ground. For about the first half of the 1900s, miniature trains sped through tunnels beneath the streets of Chicago. But these railroad cars didn't carry people—they moved cargo, including coal, mail, and soil from construction projects. And they did it efficiently since they were never slowed down by traffic jams.

But times changed and the train company went bankrupt. In 1959, the tunnels were closed and are now almost forgotten.

On the tracks to the left of center, you can see one of the miniature Chicago freight cars.

experts who've examined the train car believe it could even accommodate armed guards.

People speculate that Roosevelt was carried into his automobile in the privacy of the White House grounds, where no outsiders would see him. Then that car was driven to the nearby train station—and right up onto Roosevelt's special railcar. The president wouldn't have to get out of his automobile to enter the train and there'd be no revealing photographs taken of him.

Covert Arrival Beneath the Waldorf Astoria Hotel

When Roosevelt's train arrived deep below the streets of New York, far from the crowd's and the reporters' eyes, a special rail line known as Track 61 guided it to its own private railway station. This was completely separate from the rest of New York's rail system. There, trusted staff slid a ramp up to the railcar and Roosevelt was driven off the train—already in his car.

The secret train stop was built in the 1930s, which was when Roosevelt became president. That's why people believe it was built especially for him, although other wealthy Americans who wanted to sneak in and out of New York City without being seen likely used it too. The stop was very close to a freight elevator under the Waldorf Astoria. But this wasn't just any elevator. Like Roosevelt's train car, it was large enough and strong enough to accommodate a car.

The gleaming doors of the elevator opened, and Roosevelt was driven in. Then he and his driver rode up 12 stories. The elevator's doors, ordinary and anonymous, opened right on to

the street, close to Grand Central Terminal. The president's car motored off, and Roosevelt was on his way to his next appointment. Nobody thought about the fact that they'd never seen Roosevelt get into or out of his car.

The special railcar, hidden away on an almost forgotten underground piece of track just beyond Grand Central Terminal, helped keep Roosevelt's secret safe. He strongly led his country through World War II. Some people say many other American presidents have used the mysterious subterranean station as well—and perhaps still do when they want to escape reporters and the public.

THE SECRETS REVEALED

Operation Elster: Fail

The German spies Erich Gimpel and William Colepaugh never infiltrated deeper into Grand Central Terminal than the baggage storage room. Although they didn't even get near M42, they were convicted of conspiracy and sentenced to life imprisonment.

The original converters that Gimpel and Colepaugh were trying to sabotage are still there, although in the late 1900s they were replaced by more modern ones. M42 has been shown on various television shows (and you can see videos featuring it online), but its exact location continues to be a closely guarded secret and doesn't appear on any maps. The building's owners didn't even officially acknowledge M42 until the late 1980s.

The Presidential Solution

And Roosevelt's secret train car? For years, New York commuters had wondered about the strange railcar they could sometimes glimpse through the dirt and murk as their subway clattered out of Grand Central Terminal. No one

GHOSTLY GATORS?

For years, people have told tales of huge colonies of giant albino alligators living in the sewers of New York City. They're great stories, but there are no alligators of any size or color secretly living in the tunnels beneath the city.

Alligators would last only a few months in New York's sewers, thanks to the too-cold water and the bacteria and other organisms living in it. Any gators that have crawled out of sewers are usually found to be escaped pets or runaways from aquariums or zoos.

HOGS UNDERGROUND

The construction workers who dig the tunnels for New York's subways, utilities, sewers, and more are known as "sandhogs." Workers used to explode dynamite to blow holes in the rock below the city, but today they use tunnel-boring machines (TBMs), also known as "moles."

You can find videos online of sandhogs at work. It's a tough, dangerous job, but New York depends on the tunnels and passages dug far below its busy streets.

has ever admitted that the railcar was Roosevelt's, but the car's construction, with its special glass and armor, makes the connection likely.

As well, lettering on the railcar identifies it as definitely not belonging to the railroad system but likely owned by the American government. No wonder many people still speculate about this abandoned mystery car that has rested forgotten for decades. After all, the underground track it rests on has never even appeared on maps of Grand Central Terminal.

From subterranean converters that saved the world during World War II to unidentified railcars from the same era that likely protected a president's privacy, New York City's secrets extend deep, deep underground.

Tunnel-boring machines can be many times bigger than the workers who operate them.

POLITICIANS
DEEP
DOWN

The resort that hid
a nuclear shelter

THE PLACE: THE GREENBRIER, WEST VIRGINIA

THE BIG EVENT: THE COLD WAR (1945–1991)

The massive metal door slammed shut with a thundering boom! Behind it, the concrete halls and underground rooms lay silent and still. Only a few top government officials knew the chambers even existed. Two trusted staffers were now walking away from the quiet darkness.

Built quickly—desperately—to house hundreds of important American politicians, the secret subterranean bunker was always totally equipped and ready. Or so the American government hoped.

Rows of bunk beds waited for sleepers—but no one had ever even dozed there. A fully equipped hospital stood prepared to treat its first patient. Guns and batons in the security room hung ready to protect the underground bunker from invaders.

Gradually the footsteps faded away, leaving the top-secret bunker in inky belowground blackness. Waiting.

THE BEGINNINGS UNCOVERED

The Cold War Heats Up

President Dwight D. Eisenhower was worried. Very worried. As a hero of World War II, he knew how war could devastate whole countries. Surely nations would never want to launch such horror on the world again—would they?

America had ended World War II by dropping atomic bombs on two cities in Japan. Since then, other countries, including what was then called the Soviet Union (today's Russia), had built nuclear missiles. What if one of these countries chose to use its devastating bombs?

This period of uncertainty that followed World War II was known as the Cold War, and it lasted from about 1945 to 1991. There was little actual fighting (unlike in a "hot" war, such as the Iraq War), but in speeches and announcements the United States (and its allies) and the Soviet Union (and its fellow countries) constantly complained and sniped at each other. The Cold War often seemed to be on the verge of becoming hot. Very hot.

The rivalry was based on major differences between the two superpowers. The United States felt the Soviet communist system, in which everything was owned by the community or state (not by individual people), wasn't fair. The Soviet government believed the North American capitalist system of individuals or corporations making their own profits and not having to share them was decadent and wrong.

Avoiding a Nuclear Wasteland

Many North Americans feared a Soviet missile targeted on Washington would turn their entire continent into a nuclear wasteland, covered in radioactive fallout. A blast could flatten buildings and everyone in them, blind hundreds of thousands with its brilliant light, and ignite chains of devastating fires. So during the 1950s, adults and children were taught to "duck and cover" (see page 68) under desks and tables to protect themselves.

Eisenhower decided America must prepare for nuclear war. That meant that no matter what chaos might rage through Washington,

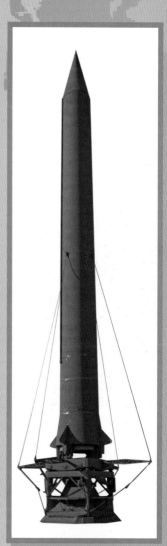

North Americans feared the Soviet Union's nuclear weapons, like this SS-4 missile.

DUCK AND COVER!

After the Soviet Union exploded its first atomic bomb in 1949, North Americans became very nervous about exposure to nuclear radiation and fallout. So they could protect themselves in case of an attack, kids were shown a film about how to duck under their school desks at the first sign of a blast, then cover their heads with their hands.

You can see the "Duck and Cover" film online. Today, kids in earthquake- and hurricane-prone areas still learn to duck and cover to protect themselves in an emergency.

DC, its congressmen and senators would be kept safe, able to govern whatever remained of the country. Eisenhower decreed that a secret underground shelter be built.

But where would be both safe enough and secret enough?

JUST THE FACTS

The Perfect Location

Eisenhower already had an idea about a good location for the government bunker—The Greenbrier, a resort near White Sulphur Springs in southern West Virginia. It was fairly close to Washington, so officials could get there quickly in case of an emergency. But it was far enough away—about a five-hour drive—that if the capital was bombed, the bunker would still be safe. Eisenhower also remembered that The Greenbrier was surrounded by mountains that might block any clouds of nuclear fallout.

The Not-So-Secret Secret

Construction of the bunker began in 1959. Immediately, there was a problem: How could the government build a huge facility without anyone else—especially foreign spies—knowing what they were doing? Instead of trying to hide the construction, which would have been impossible, they decided to do what magicians do—direct people's attention away from what they didn't want them to see.

The Greenbrier announced to the world that it was beginning a major expansion and would be building a whole new wing. What no one mentioned was what was being secretly built under the wing.

Construction workers signed documents swearing them to secrecy. However, their silence was based on much more than a promise. They were also proud that their government had chosen their area for such a special building.

Construction of The Greenbrier secret underground bunker in 1959 (left).

When construction was completed, the bunker would be hidden deep below The Greenbrier's West Virginia Wing.

Digging All Night Long

Once the immense hole was dug, construction started. Workers built long into the night, every night, to finish the underground bunker as soon as possible. No one wanted to think about how soon it might be needed. Quickly, rooms and passageways began to take shape. The outer walls were an incredible 1.5 meters (5 feet) thick and reinforced with steel. On top was a heavy concrete roof, and then at least 6.1 meters (20 feet) of soil. In some places, there was three times this amount.

Even the bunker doors were incredible. They were massive—but so carefully balanced that they could be opened or closed by just one person. One weighed more than 28 tonnes (28 tons), or more than a large city bus packed with passengers. Imagine being able to push that with just one hand!

But what was behind the doors was even more amazing.

HIDDEN

Behind the Hidden Door

When The Greenbrier's West Virginia Wing opened in 1962, people thronged to see the latest attraction at the resort. They didn't

This Florida bomb shelter was built for President John F. Kennedy in 1961.

PROTECTING THE PRESIDENT

The Greenbrier underground bunker was only for the politicians in America's Senate and House of Representatives and their aides. Before this subterranean hideaway was built, the country already had secret command posts for the president, vice president, and Supreme Court.

Even today, no one knows for sure where they are, but they're likely on the east coast, carved deep into mountains there. And they're probably still carefully hidden and maintained.

realize that the massive new "Exhibit Hall" was actually part of the bunker. The room could be sealed off in seconds, and behind a decorative screen in a corner was one of the bunker's vast doors.

In a nuclear emergency, staff would rush the politicians through the door as soon as they arrived from Washington. The entrance would slam shut immediately. Then the officials would be quickly led into a large decontamination room, with its stark tiled walls and multiple showerheads. Anyone arriving at the bunker after a nuclear bomb attack might have been contaminated by deadly radioactive fallout, and it would be vital to remove it as rapidly as possible.

So the officials would quickly strip off all their clothes (which would be burned, along with their wallets, purses, and more) and pass under high-power showers to wash off the dangerous dust. Then the politicians would receive a uniform of clean coveralls and finally be allowed to enter the main bunker.

The bunker had to accommodate the country's congressmen and senators, as well as one assistant each, which added up to more than 1,000 people. The facility's 153 rooms sprawled over almost 1.2 hectares (3 acres), or a space about the size of two football fields stacked on top of each other. Here, the politicians would sleep, eat, and work for as long as necessary—or as long as possible.

Day-to-Day Living—and Dying

The dormitories were far belowground—and far below the standards these pampered politicians were used to. Every dormitory could sleep 60 people in bare metal bunk beds with thin mattresses. Rows and rows of beds lined the walls. One government official who toured the bunker in the 1960s said, "I remember the first time I saw it, especially the dormitory. I had bad dreams that night. It's one of those experiences you don't lightly forget."

Cartons of long-lasting food rations lined one of the bunker's long tunnels.

About 400 people could eat at the same time in the bunker's cafeteria, with its black-and-white checked floors, orangey-red walls, and blue vinyl chairs. The windows looked out on fresh, lush country. But wait—this cafeteria was underground, so how could its windows show views of anything but dirt? Actually, they were paintings, not windows, created so the politicians would feel as if they were still aboveground.

The meals served in the cafeteria were definitely less than gourmet! They had to be made from food that didn't require refrigeration and could last a long time in case all the food outside was too radioactive to be brought in. So the food was prepackaged and sealed, like the rations soldiers eat. There was enough to feed the bunker's entire population for two months. Planners hoped that after that they would be able to find food outside the bunker.

There were many meeting rooms, but there was also a

Each of the bunker's 18 dormitories was built to sleep 60 politicians in rows of bunk beds.

BACKYARD BUNKERS

It's hard now to imagine what life was like when the Cold War was at its worst. In the early 1960s, many North Americans went to bed wondering if they'd be incinerated before the next dawn.

Some communities built public fallout shelters. People created basement hideaways or dug underground bomb shelters in their backyards. Parents filled them with canned food so their families could survive if they were stuck underground for weeks. Others moved to Australia, figuring that "down under" they'd be safe from nuclear warfare in the planet's northern hemisphere.

This fallout shelter includes a 14-day supply of food and water, battery-operated radio, first aid kit, and more.

library and a place where people might relax—if they could. With its rug and padded chairs, this room looked like a downscale waiting room, but was probably the coziest place in the bunker.

The bunker even had a hospital with an operating room. There was a supply of prescription medicines and spare eyeglasses for the politicians. If someone died, the body would be transported to the "pathological waste incinerator"—in other words, a place where cremations could be done. It was the only way to dispose of bodies, since burying them outside wouldn't be possible.

A huge multistory power plant supplied all the buried bunker's heating, air-conditioning, and electrical needs. A confusion of pipes, tubes, and vats stretched off in all directions, while thousands of gauges and valves hummed and clicked. The plant was designed to provide enough power for 1,100 people to live there for 40 days. There were also immense water tanks, as well as tanks full of diesel fuel for the bunker's engines. Air had to be filtered and cooled to try to keep it as fresh and clean as possible.

Broadcasting to the Nation

Of course, the politicians would need to keep in touch with any citizens out there in the nuclear wasteland, so deep in the bunker was a television studio. While speaking to what was left of the nation, top officials would stand in front of a photograph that showed the dome of Washington's Capitol building surrounded by leafy trees. No matter how the city really looked at that moment, the picture would give Americans the message that everything was just fine.

An entrance dug down into

the ground covering the bunker could be opened to reveal the eight-story-high transmission tower that would allow the officials to broadcast to their devastated nation. In case of a disaster, no one knew what might land on top of this door, so it was strong enough to lift 5 tonnes (5 tons) of dirt and rubble as it pushed open.

On Guard!

Security cameras scanned the woods and hills around the buried bunker, on constant alert to detect intruders. There was also a weapon room, filled with guns, batons, and riot gear so that bunker police could keep the facility safe and secret.

Besides the bunker door off the Exhibit Hall, another entrance was hidden in the woods behind the new wing, camouflaged with forest-green paint and a sign that said Danger High Voltage. There wasn't actually any electrical charge to beware of there, but the sign warned off curious investigators—and spies.

Behind another huge door was a long tunnel where trucks rumbled down into the bunker with supplies, fuel, and equipment. The gray concrete walls leading into the bunker were sterile and bleak, lined with a network of metal pipes and lit by harsh overhead lighting.

"We're Just Here to Fix the Cable"

Since some government officials believed a nuclear disaster could strike at any time, once the subterranean bunker was built, the fuel, food, medications—even the magazines—were kept in a constant state of readiness. You'd think the local people might notice staff going back and forth maintaining the bunker. But the government had figured out a way to keep the maintenance a secret.

The Greenbrier had a company that looked after all its televisions and cable services. And that was all the company did—supposedly.

Actually, the company spent just a fraction of its time looking after the resort's TV needs. The rest of the time the employees looked after the underground bunker, keeping the communication equipment current, moving out food that was past its best-before date, and more. Once a week, after most of the regular staff at

TUNNELS AND TOMBS

Boston, Massachusetts, is another important city in America's wartime history, especially the city's North End and the Old North Church. Below the church are tombs and crypts, while tunnels connect homes and shops in the neighbourhood.

Long ago these abandoned tunnels were all used by smugglers. During the American Revolution, soldiers hid in the tunnels and supplies were stored here. Much later, in 1950, those same tunnels may have played a part in a robbery that was the largest armed robbery in the United States up to that point!

The Greenbrier had left for the day, special workers snuck down into the bunker and tested the diesel generators in the power plant.

High Alert

The closest The Greenbrier bunker ever came to being used was shortly after it was completed in October 1962 during the Cuban Missile Crisis. This confrontation pitted Cuba and the Soviet Union against the United States.

Nikita Khrushchev (left) and John F. Kennedy meeting in 1961.

The United States discovered that Cuba was building sites for nuclear missiles. When the U.S. saw Soviet warships carrying nuclear missiles steaming toward Cuba, it announced it would set up a blockade to stop the ships. Tensions were especially high when several Soviet ships tried to run the blockade. People around the world held their breath wondering what would happen next; for days it seemed as though neither U.S. President John F. Kennedy nor Nikita Khrushchev, the leader of the Soviet Union, would back down.

The bunker under The Greenbrier was on high alert. Staff rushed to prepare for what seemed like the inevitable arrival of politicians. In the dead of night, trucks with vital deliveries roared up to the huge doors. The bunker stood ready to receive Washington's congressmen and senators on a moment's notice.

The world teetered on the brink of disaster—nuclear war had become a very real possibility. At the last minute, America and the Soviet Union reached a compromise. The Soviets agreed to take all the weapons on the warships and in Cuba back to the Soviet Union. The U.S. promised never to invade Cuba and to remove U.S.-built nuclear weapons from countries close to the Soviet Union.

The whole world heaved a sigh of relief. The Cuban Missile Crisis was over. Staff at the bunker was finally once again able to stand down.

Years passed. The Greenbrier bunker remained unused but ready for service. Its secret was still safe.

One of the entrances to Colorado's Cheyenne Mountain Complex.

THE SECRET REVEALED

The Case of the Curious Journalist

In the end, it wasn't anyone from White Sulphur Springs who told the world about the subterranean bunker. It was a curious outsider. In the early 1990s, American journalist Ted Gup checked into The Greenbrier. But he wasn't there to relax and play golf.

Gup had heard rumors about the underground government shelter and now he wanted answers. While everyone he talked to at the hotel denied knowing anything about the secret compound, Gup kept digging for information.

On May 31, 1992, Gup published an article in *The Washington Post* that completely exposed the bunker. The subterranean secret that had been kept for more than three decades was finally revealed. Some people branded Gup as a traitor for giving away the secret.

The day after the story was published and the secret was revealed, the bunker was immediately phased out. Almost all the

MORE BURIED GOVERNMENT SECRETS

The Greenbrier bunker may be open to the public now, but many people believe there are still lots of secret underground government bunkers across the United States. Some of these military bases and other complexes are several levels deep and as big as large cities.

The Cheyenne Mountain Complex in Colorado can withstand multimegaton attacks. In Pennsylvania, the Raven Rock Mountain Complex is known as the Underground Pentagon. The High Point Special Facility near Bluemont, Virginia, was hollowed out of solid rock.

equipment and furniture hidden deep underground was removed and dispersed to other government buildings.

By 1995, The Greenbrier began offering tours of its no-longer-secret bunker. In 2002, companies began storing important electronic records in the converted belowground dormitories—or at least that's the story that tour guides tell curious tourists about mysterious locked areas.

Would the Bunker Have Worked?

The bunker might have been useful back in the 1960s, when the United States government would have had hours of warning of an impending nuclear attack. But as years went by, those hours shrunk to minutes or less. Eventually weapons could be set off so quickly that there would have been no way so many elected officials could be transported from Washington to the underground refuge in so little time.

This door to The Greenbrier secret bunker weighs 25 tonnes (25 tons).

NUCLEAR TOURISM

You can now tour the bunker at The Greenbrier. There, you'll slip behind the massive doors and go back in time into the communications area, cafeteria, and more. There is also a dormitory set up with rows of bunk beds, with the bedding neatly arranged under plastic coverings. A video will tell you about the Cold War, and in the exhibition gallery you'll see historic artifacts and photos.

People can even rent the bunker for parties—they can choose between an army camp hospital or spy theme!

Another problem with the buried bunker was that the politicians could each bring a staff member into the bunker but would have had to leave their families behind. How many of the officials would have been willing to abandon their spouses and kids, not knowing how they were suffering in a post-atomic world full of unimaginable horrors?

Journalist Gup argued that he'd performed a service to the government; he'd exposed a facility that was no longer functional.

The Cold War ended in 1991 after improved relations between the Soviet Union and the United States in the late 1980s and finally the collapse of the Soviet Union. It all happened just a year before the secret of The Greenbrier bunker was revealed. If it weren't for Ted Gup's article, the subterranean bunker would probably still be kept at the ready.

But many people believe that somewhere in the U.S. another bunker is ready and waiting, buried safely deep underground, just in case …

Signs like this one marked the locations of fallout shelters during the Cold War.

TIME LINE

1300s

1325   Aztecs found city of Tenochtitlán

1500s

August 13, 1521   Hernán Cortés and his conquistadors destroy most of Tenochtitlán and conquer city

1800s

January 24, 1848   California Gold Rush begins when gold is found at Sutter's Mill, California

1855   California Gold Rush ends

April 12, 1861   American Civil War begins (in South Carolina)

May 23, 1862   Battle of Lewisburg in West Virginia; after, Southern troops rest in Organ Cave

1863   Confederate troops abandon Organ Cave

April 9, 1865   American Civil War ends

1900s

1903   Moose Jaw, Saskatchewan, linked to a rail line heading north from Chicago

1918   Prohibition begins in Canada

1920   Prohibition begins in United States

1930   Prohibition ends in most of Canada

1933   Prohibition ends in United States

September 1, 1939	World War II begins when Germany and Slovakia attack Poland
December 8, 1941	United States enters World War II
November 29, 1944	Nazis Erich Gimpel and William Colepaugh land in Bar Harbor, Maine
August 14, 1945	Japan surrenders and World War II ends
1945	Cold War begins
1959	Construction of The Greenbrier bunker in West Virginia begins
October 1962	Construction of The Greenbrier bunker in West Virginia completed
October 1962	Cuban Missile Crisis
1970s	Moose Jaw, Saskatchewan, tunnels rediscovered
February 25, 1978	Templo Mayor uncovered in Mexico City
December 1991	Cold War ends
May 31, 1992	*The Washington Post* exposes The Greenbrier bunker

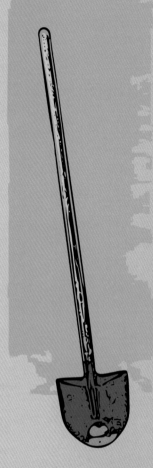

2000s

October 1, 2006	Archaeologists discover huge carved stone at Templo Mayor in Mexico City
October 6, 2011	Archaeologists find Aztec ceremonial platform studded with carved serpent heads at Templo Mayor in Mexico City

PLACES TO VISIT

To find more information on any of these sites, you can look them up on the Internet.

Spanish Conquest

Chapultepec Park, Mexico City, Mexico
Templo Mayor Museum, Mexico City, Mexico

Gold Rush

Gold Rush Museum, San Francisco, CA
Museum of the City of San Francisco, San Francisco, CA
San Francisco History Museum, San Francisco, CA
Sutter's Fort State Historic Park, Sacramento, CA

American Civil War

American Civil War Museum, Gettysburg, PA
Civil War Museum, Kenosha, WI
Confederate Memorial Hall Museum, New Orleans, LA
Gettysburg National Military Park, Gettysburg, PA
Organ Cave, Ronceverte, WV
Petersburg National Battlefield Park, Petersburg, VA
The National Civil War Museum, Harrisburg, PA

Prohibition

Chicago History Museum, Chicago, IL
National Museum of Crime & Punishment, Washington, DC
Tunnels of Moose Jaw, Moose Jaw, Saskatchewan, Canada

World War II

Canadian War Museum, Ottawa, Ontario, Canada
The National WWII Museum, New Orleans, LA

Cold War

The Bunker at The Greenbrier, White Sulphur Springs, WV
Diefenbunker, Carp, Ontario, Canada

MAIN SOURCES

Spanish Conquest

David Saul. *War: From Ancient Egypt to Iraq.* New York: Dorling Kindersley, 2009.

Jacques Soustelle. *Daily Life of the Aztecs on the Eve of the Spanish Conquest.* Stanford, CA: Stanford University Press, 1910.

Gold Rush

J. S. Holliday. *Rush for Riches: Gold Fever and the Making of California.* Berkeley, CA: University of California Press, 1999.

Liza Ketchum. *The Gold Rush.* Boston: Little, Brown and Company, 1996.

Civil War

Allen C. Guelzo. *Fateful Lightning: A New History of the Civil War & Reconstruction.* New York: Oxford University Press, 2012.

John Keegan. *The American Civil War.* New York: Alfred A. Knopf, 2009.

Christopher J. Olsen. *The American Civil War.* New York: Hill and Wang, 2006.

Thomas E. Woods. *33 Questions About American History You're Not Supposed to Ask.* New York: Crown Forum, 2007.

Prohibition

Edward Behr. *Prohibition: Thirteen Years That Changed America.* New York: Arcade Publishing, 1996.

James H. Gray. *Booze: When Whisky Ruled the West.* Saskatoon, SK: Fifth House Publishers, 1995.

William J. Helmer and Arthur J. Bilek. *The St. Valentine's Day Massacre.* Nashville: Cumberland House, 2004.

Peter S. Li. *The Chinese in Canada.* Toronto: Oxford University Press, 1998.

Ormond Knight McKague. *Racism in Canada.* Saskatoon, SK: Fifth House Publishers, 1991.

Daniel Okrent. *Last Call: The Rise and Fall of Prohibition.* New York: Scribner, 2010.

Gord Steinke. *Mobsters & Rumrunners of Canada.* Edmonton, AB: Folklore Publishing, 2003.

World War II

William B. Breuer. *The Spy Who Spent the War in Bed.* Hoboken, NJ: John Wiley & Sons, 2003.

Erich Gimpel. *Agent 146.* New York: Thomas Dunne Books, 2003.

Cold War

Michael F. Hopkins. *The Cold War.* New York: Thames & Hudson Inc., 2011.

Robert J. McMahon. *The Cold War.* Oxford, UK: Oxford University Press, 2003.

Priscilla Roberts. *The Cold War.* Stroud, UK: Sutton Publishing Ltd., 2000.

Merrilyn Thomas. *The Cold War.* Oxford, UK: Oneworld Publications, 2009.

FURTHER READING

Spanish Conquest

Elizabeth Baquedano. *Aztec, Inca & Maya.* New York: Dorling Kindersley, 2005.

Tim Cooke. *Ancient Aztec: Archaeology Unlocks the Secrets of Mexico's Past.* Washington: National Geographic Society, 2007.

Laurie Coulter. *Ballplayers and Bonesetters: One Hundred Ancient Aztec and Maya Jobs You Might Have Adored or Abhorred.* Toronto: Annick Press, 2008.

Terry Deary. *Amazing Aztecs.* Toronto: Scholastic Canada, 2010.

Nicholas Saunders and Tony Allan. *The Aztec Empire.* Chicago: Heinemann Library, 2005.

Michael Schuman. *Maya and Aztec Mythology Rocks!* Berkeley Heights, NJ: Enslow Publishers, 2011.

Gold Rush

Brian Belval. *Gold.* New York: Rosen Publishing Group, 2007.

Barbara Greenwood. *Gold Rush Fever: A Story of the Klondike, 1898.* Toronto: Kids Can Press, 2001.

Stuart A. Kallen and P. M. Boekhoff. *The Gold Rush.* San Diego, CA: Kidhaven Press, 2002.

Marc Tyler Nobleman. *The Klondike Gold Rush.* Minneapolis, MN: Compass Point Books, 2006.

Rosalyn Schanzer. *Gold Fever! Tales from the California Gold Rush.* Washington: National Geographic Society, 1999.

Civil War

American Civil War. Chicago: World Book, Inc., 2011.

Christopher Collier. *The Civil War, 1860–1865.* New York: Benchmark Books, 2000.

Stuart Kallen. *The Civil War and Reconstruction.* Edina, MN: Abdo & Daughters, 2001.

James M. McPherson. *Fields of Fury: The American Civil War.* New York: Atheneum Books for Young Readers, 2002.

John E. Stanchak. *Civil War.* New York: Dorling Kindersley, 2000.

Prohibition

Mary Harelkin Bishop. *Tunnels of Time: A Moose Jaw Adventure.* Regina, SK: Coteau Books, 2000.

Karen Blumenthal. *Bootleg: Murder, Moonshine, and the Lawless Years of Prohibition.* New York: Roaring Brook Press, 2011.

Tom Stockdale. *Life and Times of Al Capone.* New York: Chelsea House Publishers, 1997.

Richard Worth. *Teetotalers and Saloon Smashers: The Temperance Movement and Prohibition.* Berkeley Heights, NJ: Enslow Publishers, 2009.

World War II

Simon Adams. *World War II.* New York: Dorling Kindersley, 2007.

Reg Grant. *World War II: The Events and Their Impact on Real People.* New York: Dorling Kindersley, 2008.

Elizabeth MacLeod. *Eleanor Roosevelt.* Toronto: Kids Can Press, 2006.

Stuart Murray. *World War II.* Long Island City, NY: Hammond World Atlas, 2009.

Mike Taylor. *Leaders of World War II.* Edina, MN: Abdo & Daughters, 1998.

Cold War

Simon Adams. *The Cold War.* North Mankato, MN: Sea-to-Sea Publications, 2005.

Leila M. Foster. *The Cold War.* Chicago: Childrens Press Inc., 1990.

R. G. Grant. *The Cold War.* London, UK: Arcturus Publishing, 2008.

PHOTO CREDITS

INDEX

radioactive fallout, 67, 70. *See also* fallout, nuclear warfare
railcars, 61, 62, 63, 64
railroads, 41, 42, 46, 47, 56, 62, 63, 64, 78
Raven Rock Mountain Complex, 75
Roosevelt, Franklin D., 60–64
Rotten Row, 21
rumrunning, 46, 50
Russia. *See* Soviet Union

saber-toothed cats, 31, 37
sabotage, 55, 56, 57, 63
sailors, 16, 20, 22
saltpeter, 32, 33, 35
San Francisco, 16–26, 80
sandhogs, 64
Saskatchewan, 40–45, 47–52, 78, 79, 80
Seattle, Washington, 26
secrets, 14, 25, 26, 54, 56, 58, 60, 62, 63, 64, 66, 75
senate, 44, 70
senators, 68, 70, 74
sewers, 63, 64
Sherman, William, 38
ships, 11, 16, 18–26, 46, 55, 74
slavery, 29
sloths, giant ground, 31
smallpox, 10
smuggling, 32, 46, 48, 73
Snowbirds, the, 41
soldiers, 4, 7, 28, 29, 30–35, 37, 54, 55, 57, 73
South Africa, 24
South America, 6, 19
Southerners, 28, 29, 31, 32, 34, 35, 38, 78
Soviet Union, 67, 68, 74, 77
Spain, 7
Spanish Conquest, 4–14, 80
speakeasies, 38, 46
spies, 28, 54, 55, 57, 58, 59, 63, 68, 73, 76
St. Lawrence Seaway, 11
stalactites, 36
stalagmites, 36
subways, 14, 25, 56, 63, 64
Sutter, John, 17
Sutter's Mill, 17, 18, 78, 80

temples, 4, 6, 7, 11, 12, 14
Templo Mayor, 6, 11, 12, 13, 14, 79, 80
Tenochtitlán, 4–14, 78
Thornton, Illinois, 52
Toronto, 21
Track 61, 62
trains, 25, 38, 54, 55, 56, 58, 60, 61, 62, 63
Transamerica Pyramid, 24
Tulsa, Oklahoma, 47
tunnel-boring machines (TBMs), 64
tunnels, 22, 28, 31, 34, 35, 37, 38, 40–45, 47, 48–52, 58, 60, 61, 62, 63, 64, 71, 73, 79, 80

Union Army, 28, 29, 34, 35, 38
United States, 6, 16–38, 41, 42, 43, 44, 45, 47, 50, 54–77, 78, 79. *See also* America

Virginia, 34, 75, 80

Waldorf Astoria, the, 61, 62
war, 5, 7, 25, 28–38, 54–61, 63, 64, 66–77, 78, 79, 80
War of 1812, 35
Washington, 67, 68, 70, 72, 74, 76, 80
West Virginia, 28–38, 66, 68–77, 78, 79, 80
White House, 62
White Sulphur Springs, 68, 75, 80
women, 20, 44, 45, 46, 57
Women's Christian Temperance Union (W.C.T.U.), 45
World War II, 54–61, 63, 64, 67, 79, 80

Yucatan, 6

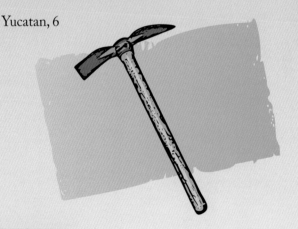